WILDFLOWERS

The Macmillan Field Guide Series includes

Birds of North America: Eastern Region

Astronomy: A Step-by-Step Guide to the Night Sky

Rocks and Minerals

Wildflowers of North America

Fossils

Weather and Forecasting

Mushrooms of North America (forthcoming)

Trees of North America (forthcoming)

Birds of North America: Western Region (forthcoming)

MACMILLAN FIELD GUIDES

WILDFLOWERS

A Quick Identification Guide
to the Wildflowers
of North America

by

Robert H. Mohlenbrock

COLLIER BOOKS
Macmillan Publishing Company, New York
Collier Macmillan Publishers, London

On the cover: Smooth Phlox, *Phlox glaberrima* (page 96).
Photograph by Robert H. Mohlenbrock.

Macmillan Publishing Company
866 Third Avenue, New York, N.Y. 10022
Collier Macmillan Canada, Inc.

Library of Congress Cataloging-in-Publication Data

Mohlenbrock, Robert H., 1931 –
  Wildflowers.

  (Macmillan field guides)
  Bibliography: p.
  Includes index.
  1. Wild flowers—United States—Identification.
2. Wild flowers—Canada—Identification. I. Title.
II. Series.
QK115.M58 1987   582.13'097   86-21614

ISBN 0-02-063420-X

Macmillan books are available at special discounts for bulk purchases for sales
promotions, premiums, fund-raising, or educational use. For details, contact:

Special Sales Director
Macmillan Publishing Company
866 Third Avenue
New York, N.Y. 10022

10 9 8 7 6 5 4 3 2 1

The Macmillan Field Guide Series: Wildflowers is also published
in a hardcover edition by Macmillan Publishing Company.

Printed in the United States of America

Acknowledgments

There are several people I wish to acknowledge who assisted me in some aspect of this book. To all the photographers who sent me thousands of excellent photos of wildflowers, I extend my thanks. Credits for photographs chosen appear at the end of the book. I am indebted to those who assisted me in determining what species should be included in the book. These include Robert Auge, Seattle, Wash.; Richard Brewer, Kalamazoo, Mich.; Thomas Elias, Claremont, Calif.; George Folkerts, Auburn, Ala.; Paul J. Harmon, Milford, Ohio; Thomas Heineke, Memphis, Tenn.; William Hopkins, Bend, Ore.; Steve Huston, Tishomingo, Okla.; Roger Johnson, Somerville, N.J.; Steve Jones, Clemson, S.C.; Doug Ladd, St. Louis, Mo.; Davis McGregor, Clemson, S.C.; Steve Olson, Carbondale, Ill.; Steve Orzell, Austin, Tex.; Annette Parker, Baton Rouge, La.; Lawrence Stritch, Pittsfield, Ill.; Robert Tatina, Mitchell, S.D.; W. Carl Taylor, Milwaukee, Wis.; Eric Ulaszek, Champaign, Ill.; Rob Wikel, Crete, Neb.; Donald Windler, Towson, Md.; A. H. Winward, Ogden, Utah; and Michael Woods, Carbondale, Ill.

I am pleased to acknowledge my wife, Beverly, and our three children, Mark, Wendy, and Trent, who have spent many years accompanying me on countless field trips. My wife typed the drafts of the manuscript, and my son Mark prepared the illustrated glossary. To them I am grateful.

Without the critical eye and friendly suggestions of Michael E. Agnes, my editor at Macmillan, this book would not be what it is. I offer him my very special thanks.

Robert H. Mohlenbrock

Contents

Preface   9

Introduction
   Names and Classification   11
   How to Use This Book   12

Sequence of Plates   19

Plate Descriptions   20

Families of Flowering Plants   172

Appendixes
   Collecting and Cultivating Wildflowers   187
   Wildflower Societies   189
   Glossary   191
   Further Reading   193

Index   194

Credits   202

About the Author   203

Preface

Much of the pleasure I get out of life lies in observing the things around me. People, birds, furry animals, trees, wildflowers, and rocks have always held a fascination for me, and knowing their names fosters a special intimacy with each of them.

This book is written for anyone who wishes to learn about the most commonly encountered wildflowers in North America. Once these wildflowers have become familiar and the basic principles of identification have been mastered, more technical manuals may be consulted to identify the less common flowering plants.

Identifying all the flowering plants in North America is a formidable task that no one has been able to accomplish. Recent estimates of the number of species of flowering plants in North America north of Mexico are in excess of 20,600 species in 254 different families. For this book I have selected 304 of the most common wildflowers that grow without cultivation. These 304 plants belong to 69 different families.

Included in this book are herbaceous (that is, non-woody) plants that usually have conspicuous flowers. Not covered are trees, shrubs, and woody vines, even though most of these plants do produce flowers and are classified as flowering plants by botanists. Also excluded are many very common non-woody plants that have obscure flowers, such as grasses, sedges, and rushes.

Although many of the plants illustrated in this book are native North American species, others have been introduced from Europe or Asia or South America and have adapted themselves well to the North American climate. Plants such as the ox-eye daisy and white clover, although very common in many parts of North America, were apparently introduced by early settlers to this continent.

Flowering plants may be found on almost any landform on our continent, from the highest mountaintops to the inhospitable desert below sea level in Death Valley, from the subtropical Everglades of southern Florida to the icy tundra of the Arctic. The common plants described and illustrated in this book may be found on a leisurely hike in the woods or seen from a car window along our vast system of roads. They are there for our enjoyment—dazzling examples of our continent's precious natural resources.

Introduction

Names and Classification

Plants are often called by two types of names. Common names are those given by the local people in an area. The common name of a given plant may differ in different parts of the continent; conversely, the same common name may be applied to different plants in different areas. Thus, Klamath weed of the Pacific Northwest is called perforate St. John's-wort east of the Mississippi River. The foul-smelling species of the eastern United States known locally as skunk cabbage is not the same plant that is called skunk cabbage in western North America, and the common name "sweet william" has been applied to at least six different species of plants in North America. The common names given for the plants in this book are the ones used most frequently in the various state and regional manuals surveyed.

Every plant also has a scientific name, composed of two Latin words. The first word is the name of the genus (plural, *genera*); the second word is the species name. Plants that are very closely related are placed in the same genus, and all bear the same genus name. Thus, all the different kinds of milkweeds are in the genus *Asclepias*. Each species bears its own unique species name. The horsetail milkweed, for example, is called *Asclepias verticillata,* the butterfly milkweed is known as *Asclepias tuberosa,* and the swamp milkweed is *Asclepias incarnata.* (When several different species in the same genus are under discussion, the genus name is often abbreviated to its first letter, for example, *A. incarnata.*) Throughout the world, these three kinds of milkweeds are known by these same Latin names. This uniformity eliminates the potential confusion that variable common names can cause. Botanists who give plants their scientific names are called plant taxonomists, and they are guided by an established set of rules describing the proper procedure for naming plants.

Just as similar species are placed in the same genus, so are similar genera placed in the same family. Sunflowers, asters, daisies, and goldenrods are each different enough to be placed in their own genera, but they are also similar enough to be grouped together with the aster family. Likewise, day lily, turk's-cap lily, white trillium, wild hyacinth, and Solomon's seal are in separate genera, but they all share similar characteristics that place them in the lily family.

This book includes summaries of the characteristics and representative genera of 69 of the more common families of flowering plants in North America. These summaries appear immediately after the descriptions and illustrations of individual wildflowers. A careful reading of these family descriptions can be very useful to wildflower identification. Once you have learned the basic features of a family, it is often easy to place a particular plant in its proper family. Correct assignment of a species to its family will enable you to use other field manuals, which are often organized by family.

How to Use This Book

All you need to begin wildflower identification is a good manual like this one and the desire to observe the plants around you. No fancy equipment is necessary, and for the wildflowers included in this book, not even a magnifying glass or hand lens is essential.

The information provided in this book is designed to allow identification if you follow a few simple steps. First, check the color of the flower petals, then determine the flower's symmetry, or shape. Color and symmetry categories are prominently displayed on the text pages facing the color photographs. Next, count the number of petals or petal-like parts and note if they are separated from each other or united to some degree to form a cup, bowl, tube, or funnel. In some instances, it may be necessary to count the number of pollen-producing stamens. Necessary data on petals and stamens accompany the captions to the photographs. Finally, read the description of the species you are considering, noting features of the leaves, stems, habitat, and range.

Begin with the flower, the reproductive organ of a flowering plant. Botanists who have studied and worked in the field for many years can sometimes identify a plant at any stage in its development. For the novice, however, it is essential to have the flower of the mature plant present. Botanists have found that the flower is the plant's most stable structure—that is, over a wide geographical range and a variety of environmental conditions, the characteristics of the flower change very little. Leaves, on the other hand, are more variable and consequently are less reliable for identification. Leaves growing in the shade, for example, sometimes differ in size and/or shape from those growing in open sunlight.

Petal color is the primary characteristic by which this book is organized; it is the most immediately recognized characteristic. You will find the following groupings prominently displayed at the top of each page of descriptions: white, blue–violet, pink–purple, red–orange, and yellow. The last plates cover flowers with other colors and without petals.

Although color is the most obvious characteristic, it is not totally reliable, and variations in color need to be watched for. Beehive cactus, for example, may have pink, white, or yellow petals. Pink evening primrose is usually white when the flower first opens but becomes pink as it ages. These variations are noted in the text. Color is also a relatively subjective characteristic for many observers. One observer may feel strongly that a wildflower is purple, another may view it as distinctly pink or red. Be sure to consider these possibilities.

It is important to observe not only the color of petals but also how many petals there are and how they are arranged. The petals may be separated from each other ("free") or united in varying degrees to form cups, bowls, tubes, funnels, or other configurations. The symmetry of the petals constitutes the second major characteristic for identification (see the accompanying illustrations). Symmetry is said to be radial if an imaginary line can be drawn across the center of the flower in any direction and still result in two equal halves. Symmetry is bilateral if the imaginary line can be drawn in only one direction. The symmetry is listed on the plate descriptions after the petal color.

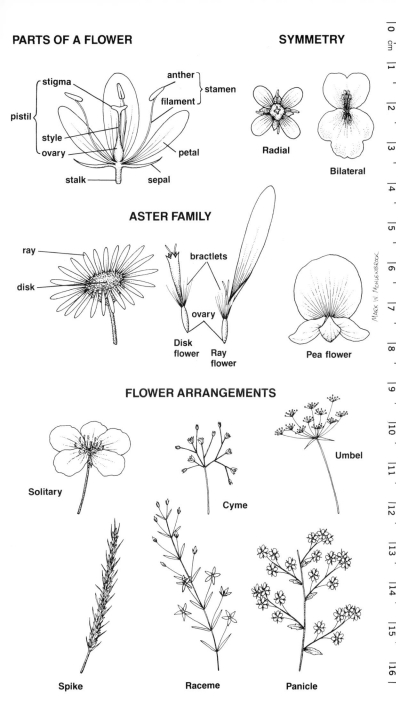

PARTS OF A FLOWER

stigma
anther
filament
stamen
pistil
style
ovary
petal
stalk
sepal

SYMMETRY

Radial

Bilateral

ASTER FAMILY

ray

disk

bractlets

ovary

Disk flower

Ray flower

Pea flower

FLOWER ARRANGEMENTS

Solitary

Cyme

Umbel

Spike

Raceme

Panicle

MACK W. MOHLENBROCK

In this book, wildflowers in the aster family are grouped together under each color heading and are thus separate from the symmetry groupings (see the Sequence of Plates on page 19). Characteristics of plants in this family are discussed elsewhere in this introduction.

Flowers may be borne at the end of a stem or arise in the junction (axil) between leaves and the stem. If there is only one flower at a given place, it is said to be solitary. In many plants there are several flowers in a cluster, or inflorescence. Basic types of clusters are umbels, spikes, racemes, and panicles; these are shown in the accompanying illustrations. In an umbel, all the flowers are on stalks that arise from a common plant, resembling the spokes of an umbrella. When the flowers are borne in an elongated row, the cluster is a spike if the flowers lack individual stalks or a raceme if each flower has its own stalk. A panicle is a compound raceme.

Surrounding the petals is usually a whorl of green sepals. Sometimes the sepals may be petal-like in color and texture, particularly if the flower lacks true petals. When it is convenient to refer to the petals and sepals together, the term *perianth* is often used. This is particularly useful when the petals and sepals are scarcely distinguishable from each other, as in lilies and orchids. At the base of some flowers, either next to the sepals or a short distance below them, may be one or more very reduced leaves called bracts.

Inward from the petals toward the center of the flower are the stamens and pistils. The stamens are composed of a slender stalk, called the filament, and an anther, where the pollen grains are formed. Counting the number of stamens in a flower is often useful in identifying a plant; in such cases the necessary data are indicated in the caption accompanying each photograph. At the center of the flower are one or more pistils, where the immature seeds develop.

The aster family, because of its unusual flower arrangements, requires special attention. The aster family is large and diverse, containing such seemingly dissimilar plants as sunflowers, goldenrods, daisies, ragweeds, dandelions, thistles, and hundreds of others. These plants are placed in the same family because their flowers are densely crowded around a single axis into a head, called a receptacle. There may be two basic flowers in a head. The flowers in the outer ring are called ray flowers; they are usually flat and often notched at the tip. The flowers in the center of the head are called disk flowers; they are tubular and elongated and often have five lobes at the tip. A daisy has both kinds of these flowers, but some species in the aster family have only ray flowers, and others have only disk flowers. Below each flower head, and closely pressed to the head, are one or more series of tiny, green, leaf-like structures called bracts.

Although the presence of flowers is essential to identification, the leaves of a plant provide additional characteristics that help clinch the identification. It is important to observe whether leaves alternate with each other on the stem or whether they grow directly opposite each other. In some plants they may grow three or more at a single point on the stem (whorled). If a leaf is a single unit, it is called a simple leaf: A leaf divided into several small leaves (leaflets) is a compound leaf. Each leaf or leaflet may be smooth-edged, or it may have teeth or deeper indentations known as lobes. Leaves may or may not be covered with minute hairs. The accompanying black-and-white illustrations show the common leaf shapes and different

LEAF STRUCTURES AND ARRANGEMENTS

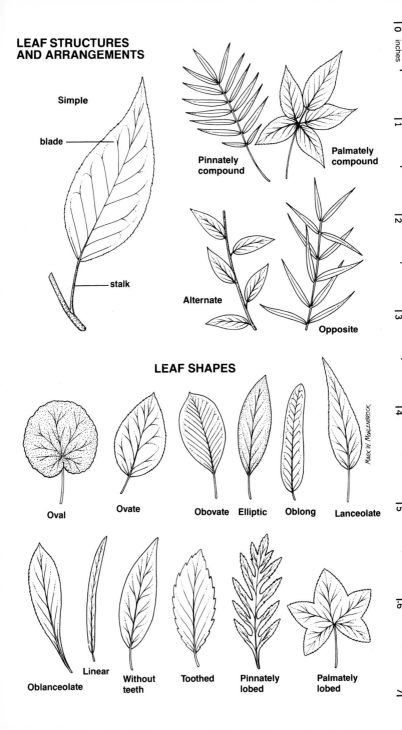

Simple

blade

stalk

Pinnately compound

Palmately compound

Alternate

Opposite

LEAF SHAPES

Oval

Ovate

Obovate

Elliptic

Oblong

Lanceolate

MARK W. MOHLENBROCK

Oblanceolate

Linear

Without teeth

Toothed

Pinnately lobed

Palmately lobed

types of leaf edges. Take time to familiarize yourself with these characteristics.

Stems, too, vary in surface features (hairy or not), arrangement (underground, upright, etc.), and height. These features are noted in the text descriptions. The succulent stems of cacti are unorthodox. They have the ability to store extraordinary quantities of water, enabling the plants to survive in arid conditions. Most cacti do not produce leaves, but many of their stems are covered with small regions called areoles, where the spines are attached. Spines that arise from the center of an areole are called central spines; those that arise from the side of the central spine are called lateral spines. It is sometimes necessary to count the number of central and lateral spines to make a positive identification of a cactus.

The species description of each wildflower in this book also includes information on the season of the year in which the plant blooms, as well as the usual habitats where it may be found. There is a code used to indicate the range of each plant in North America. The code consists of numbers and letters corresponding to those on the accompanying map. The division of North America into the regions shown on this map was proposed by the U.S. Department of Agriculture in 1982. Also listed in each description is the plant family to which the species belongs. Family summaries are given in the section immediately following the species descriptions.

Included in the comments entry for each species is information on the features that distinguish the particular species, similar species that may be confused with the plant, usefulness of the plant, and the like. Where appropriate, information on edibility may also be given. Readers who are novices at field identification are strongly cautioned to confirm identification with an expert before eating any plant.

ASTER FAMILY

Ox-eye Daisy, *Leucanthemum vulgare*

Flowers: Crowded together into 1 or a few heads up to 2″ across. Ray flowers are white, with 2–3 teeth at the tip. Disk flowers are yellow, tubular, 5-lobed. **Stems:** Smooth or sometimes hairy, to 2½′ tall. **Leaves:** Alternate, simple; lower leaves are oblong, pinnately lobed to coarsely toothed; upper leaves are narrower, coarsely toothed. **Season:** May–Oct. **Habitat:** Woods, fields, prairies. **Range** (*see map*): All areas. **Family:** Aster. **Comments:** Other members of this family with white rays and a yellow disk are dog fennel, *Anthemis cotula*, with much-divided, fern-like, ill-scented leaves; and stemless daisy, *Townsendia exscapa*, with all leaves clustered at base of plant.

Heath Aster, *Aster ericoides*

Flowers: Crowded into several heads less than 1″ across. Ray flowers number 8–20, white, about ¼″ long. Disk flowers are yellow, tubular, 5-lobed. **Stems:** Upright, hairy, to 4′ tall. **Leaves:** Alternate, simple, hairy, very small and narrow; leaves nearest the flower heads are less than ½″ long. **Season:** Sept–Nov. **Habitat:** Prairies, fields, roadsides. **Range** (*see map*): Areas 1–8, E. **Family:** Aster. **Comments:** The many other white asters found in North America include hairy aster, *A. pilosus*, with lanceolate leaves up to ½″ wide; simple aster, *A. simplex*, with nearly smooth leaves and stems; and tiny-leaved aster, *A. dumosus*, with tiny leaves near the flower heads and rays more than ¼″ long.

Annual Fleabane, *Erigeron annuus*

Flowers: Crowded together into heads up to ½″ across. Ray flowers are white, very narrow, up to 70 in number. Disk flowers are yellow, tubular. **Stems:** Upright, branched, hairy, to 4′ tall. **Leaves:** Alternate, simple, lanceolate, coarsely toothed; more than 1″ long. **Season:** June–Oct. **Habitat:** Fields, roadsides, woods. **Range** (*see map*): Areas 1–6, 9, 10, C–F. **Family:** Aster. **Comments:** Strigose fleabane, *E. strigosus*, has narrower, nearly toothless leaves and less hairy stems; spreading fleabane, *E. divergens*, has leaves less than 1″ long and stems with gray hairs.

White Layia, *Layia glandulosa*

Flowers: Crowded into a solitary head on each stem, the head up to 1½″ across. Ray flowers are white, 3-toothed at tip, usually 5–8 in number, about ⅓″ long. Disk flowers are yellow, tubular. **Stems:** Sticky and hairy, to 2′ tall. **Leaves:** Sticky and hairy; only the lower basal leaves are lobed; the upper alternate leaves are without teeth or lobes. **Season:** March–June. **Habitat:** Dry slopes, mesas. **Range** (*see map*): Areas 7–10, C. **Family:** Aster. **Comments:** Other showy layias in California include tidy tips, *L. platyglossa*, with yellow rays tipped with white and leaves with few or no lobes; Fremont's layia, *L. fremontii*, with yellow rays tipped with white and leaves with several lobes; and elegant layia, *L. elegans*, with yellow rays often bordered with white.

▲ Ox-eye Daisy
Ray and disk flowers.

▼ Heath Aster
Ray and disk flowers.

▼ Annual Fleabane
Ray and disk flowers.

▼ White Layia
Ray and disk flowers.

ASTER FAMILY

Gray Blackfoot, *Melampodium leucanthum*

Flowers: Crowded together into a few heads 1″ across. Ray flowers are white, notched at the tip, 8–10 in number. Disk flowers are yellow, tubular. **Stems:** Upright, slightly hairy, to 1½′ tall. **Leaves:** Opposite, simple, usually without teeth; gray, to 2″ long. **Season:** Jan–Dec. **Habitat:** Deserts, plains, mesas. **Range** (*see map*): Area 6. **Family:** Aster. **Comments:** The opposite, gray, nearly toothless leaves and the few inch-wide flowering heads distinguish this species. Hoary blackfoot, *M. cinereum*, has usually jagged-toothed, bright green leaves. White zinnia, *Zinnia acerosa*, with similar white heads, has only 4–6 very broad ray flowers per head.

Frostweed, *Verbesina virginica*

Flowers: Crowded together into numerous heads up to 1″ across. Ray flowers are white, less than ½″ long, not more than 5 per head. Disk flowers are white, tubular. **Stems:** Upright, hairy, with 4–5 narrow wings on the lower part, to 7′ tall. **Leaves:** Alternate, simple, ovate to lanceolate, usually toothed; somewhat rough to the touch, to 6″ long. **Season:** Aug–Nov. **Habitat:** Woods, fields, pastures. **Range** (*see map*): Areas 1–3, 5, 6. **Family:** Aster. **Comments:** The white disk and few white rays, along with the narrow wings on the lower part of the stem, distinguish this species. Wingless crownbeard, *V. encelioides*, has yellow rays and a wingless stem; winged crownbeard, *V. alternifolia*, has yellow rays, winged stems, and leaf-like structures (bracts) beneath each flower head that turn downward; sunflower crownbeard, *V. helianthoides*, has yellow rays, winged stems, and bracts beneath each flower head that do not point downward.

Milfoil (Yarrow), *Achillea millefolium*

Flowers: Crowded together into many heads in terminal clusters, each head ¼″ across. Ray flowers are white, rounded at the tip, about 6 in number. Disk flowers are pale yellow, tubular. **Stems:** Upright, smooth or hairy, to 2′ tall. **Leaves:** Alternate, deeply divided into numerous small segments, appearing fern-like; usually hairy, up to 10″ long. **Season:** May–Oct. **Habitat:** Fields, roadsides, open areas. **Range** (*see map*): All areas except B. **Family:** Aster. **Comments:** Mojave desert star, *Monoptilon bellioides*, a beautiful desert annual, has flower heads ¾″ across with about 20 rays and a yellow disk.

Feverfew, *Parthenium integrifolium*

Flowers: Crowded together into several heads up to ½″ across. Ray flowers are white, only ¹⁄₁₀″ long. Disk flowers are white, tubular. **Stems:** Upright, branched or unbranched, hairy, up to 3′ tall. **Leaves:** Alternate, simple, elliptic to lanceolate, toothed; rough and hairy to the touch, up to 8″ long and 4″ wide. **Season:** June–Sept. **Habitat:** Dry woods, prairies, glades. **Range** (*see map*): Areas 1–3, 5, 6. **Family:** Aster. **Comments:** This plant was used by the early settlers to alleviate fevers. Similar is hairy feverfew, *P. hispidum*, with long white hairs on the stem.

▲ Gray Blackfoot
Ray and disk flowers.

▲ Frostweed
Ray and disk flowers.

▲ Milfoil (Yarrow)
Ray and disk flowers.

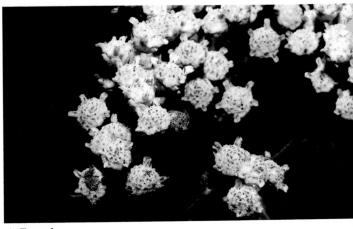

▲ Feverfew
Ray and disk flowers.

ASTER FAMILY

Pussytoes, *Antennaria plantaginifolia*

Flowers: Many, borne in terminal heads up to ⅛″ across, the pollen-bearing flowers borne on separate plants from the pistil-bearing flowers. No ray flowers. Disk flowers are white, tubular. **Stems:** Some creeping, some upright and up to 15″ tall; all with mats of cobwebby hairs. **Leaves:** Both basal and alternate, simple, ovate, without teeth; with cobwebby hairs on the lower surface, up to 3″ long and 1½″ wide. **Season:** April–June. **Habitat:** Dry woods, prairies. **Range** (*see map*): Areas 1–6, D–F. **Family:** Aster. **Comments:** Solitary pussytoes, *A. solitaria*, has only a single head at the tip of the stem.

Pearly Everlasting, *Anaphalis margaritacea*

Flowers: Crowded into numerous heads less than ½″ across. Ray flowers absent, replaced by stiff, papery, pearly white leaf-like structures (bracts). Disk flowers are yellow, tubular. **Stems:** Upright, woolly white, up to 3′ tall. **Leaves:** Alternate, simple, narrow, without teeth; woolly white, up to 5″ long. **Season:** June–Sept. **Habitat:** Open woods, often in the mountains. **Range** (*see map*): All areas except 6. **Family:** Aster. **Comments:** The pearly white, papery bracts readily distinguish this species.

RADIAL SYMMETRY

Arrowhead, *Sagittaria latifolia*

Flowers: In whorls of 3 or more, either with stamens only or pistils only, on stalks up to 2″ long. **Petals:** 3, white, separated, usually round, up to nearly 1″ long. **Stems:** Smooth, leafless, up to 5′ tall. **Leaves:** All near base of plant, usually arrowhead-shaped and up to nearly 10″ long. **Season:** July–Sept. **Habitat:** Swamps, ponds, shorelines, shallow water, mud. **Range** (*see map*): All areas except 8, A, B. **Family:** Water Plantain. **Comments:** Other common arrowheads include broad arrowhead, *S. calycina*, with inflated leaf stalks; and long-beaked arrowhead, *S. engelmanniana*, with flowers on stalks up to only 1″ long.

White Trillium, *Trillium flexipes*

Flowers: Solitary, up to 3″ across, on an arched stalk. **Petals:** 3, white, ovate. **Stems:** Upright, unbranched, smooth, up to 1½′ tall. **Leaves:** In one set of 3 just beneath the flower, simple, without teeth, pointed at the tip; smooth, up to 5″ long, nearly as wide. **Season:** April–May. **Habitat:** Moist, shaded woods. **Range** (*see map*): Areas 1–3. **Family:** Lily. **Comments:** Other white trilliums include large-flowered trillium, *T. grandiflorum*, with larger stalked flowers and stalkless leaves; nodding trillium, *T. cernuum*, with smaller stalked flowers with pink anthers; snow trillium, *T. nivale*, with stalked flowers and stalked leaves rounded at the tip; and painted trillium, *T. undulatum*, with stalked flowers and stalked leaves pointed at the tip.

▲ Pussytoes
Tubular flowers only.

▲ Pearly Everlasting
Tubular flowers only.

▲ Arrowhead
3 separated petals.

▲ White Trillium
3 separated petals.

RADIAL SYMMETRY

Sego Lily, *Calochortus nuttallii*

Flowers: Solitary or 2–4 in clusters (umbels), bell-shaped, up to 2″ across. **Petals:** 3, separated, usually white with a yellow base, with a gland surrounded by a ring of hairs, often with a purple spot above the gland. **Stems:** Upright, up to 18″ tall, smooth. **Leaves:** 1 basal leaf, smooth, up to 4″ long, narrow. **Season:** May–July. **Habitat:** Plains, open woods, dry mountains. **Range** (*see map*): Areas 4, 5, 7–10. **Family:** Lily. **Comments:** The petals in this handsome species are sometimes pink or purplish. The bulbs are edible. Sego lily is the state flower of Utah. Similar species of *Calochortus* are the large-fruited sego lily, *C. macrocarpus*, with green-striped purple petals and petal-glands surrounded by hairs; and the Gunnison sego lily, *C. gunnisonii*, with white, purple, or yellow petals and petal-glands hairy to the top.

Wild Onion, *Allium canadense*

Flowers: Several in clusters (umbels). **Petal-like Parts:** 6, all alike, separated, usually white. **Stems:** Unbranched, smooth, up to 2′ tall, with a strong odor of onion. **Leaves:** Mostly at the base of the plant, long, narrow, flat, up to ⅛″ across. **Season:** May–July. **Habitat:** Open disturbed areas, prairies. **Range** (*see map*): Areas 1–6, E, F. **Family:** Lily. **Comments:** This species differs from other wild onions by its white flowers and several narrow, flat leaves. Wild garlic, *A. vineale*, is similar but has hollow leaves; plains onion, *A. textile*, has only 2 leaves per stem, both of them flat and equaling or surpassing the stem length.

False Garlic, *Nothoscordum bivalve*

Flowers: In teminal clusters (umbels), up to ½″ long. **Petal-like Parts:** 6, separated, lanceolate. **Stems:** Smooth, up to 15″ tall. **Leaves:** All basal, flat, smooth, up to ¼″ across. **Season:** March–June, often again in Sept–Oct. **Habitat:** Dry woods, prairies, fields. **Range** (*see map*): Areas 1–3, 5, 6. **Family:** Lily. **Comments:** Although strongly resembling a wild onion, this species lacks any odor of onion.

Bride's Bonnet, *Clintonia uniflora*

Flowers: 1 per stem, up to 1½″ across. **Petal-like Parts:** 6, separated. **Stems:** Leafless, smooth, up to 6″ tall. **Leaves:** 2–3, all basal, oblong to elliptic, without teeth; smooth, up to 6″ long. **Season:** May–July. **Habitat:** Forests, particularly under conifers. **Range** (*see map*): Areas 9, 10, A, C. **Family:** Lily. **Comments:** Bride's Bonnet is distinguished by its solitary, pure white flower on a leafless stalk. It has attractive, shiny, deep blue berries. Other clintonias in North America are the speckled wood lily, *C. umbellulata*, with several white flowers speckled with green and purple; bluebead lily, *C. borealis*, with greenish yellow flowers; and Andrews' wood lily, *C. andrewsiana*, with pink to rose flowers.

▲ Wild Onion
6 separated petal-like parts.

▲ Sego Lily
3 separated petals.

▼ Bride's Bonnet
6 separated petal-like parts.

▼ False Garlic
6 separated petal-like parts.

RADIAL SYMMETRY

False Solomon's Seal, *Smilacina racemosa*

Flowers: Many, in a terminal cluster (panicle), each flower about ⅙" across. **Petal-like Parts:** 6, separated. **Stems:** Upright, smooth or hairy, up to 3' tall. **Leaves:** Alternate, simple, lanceolate to oval, pointed at the tip, without teeth; usually hairy on the lower surface, up to 6" long. **Season:** May–July. **Habitat:** Woods. **Range** (*see map*): All areas except B. **Family:** Lily. **Comments:** This is the most robust of all false Solomon's seals. Starry false Solomon's seal, *S. stellata,* has flowers in an unbranched cluster and hairy leaves; creeping false Solomon's seal, *S. trifolia,* has flowers in an unbranched cluster and smooth leaves.

Corn Lily, *Veratrum californicum*

Flowers: Many, in a dense, terminal, erect cluster up to 1½' long. **Petal-like Parts:** 6, with a green gland at the base, up to ¾" long. **Stems:** Robust, hairy, up to 8' tall. **Leaves:** Alternate, simple, ovate; up to 12" long, without stalks. **Season:** June–Aug. **Habitat:** Swamps, wet meadows, wet woods. **Range** (*see map*): Areas 7–10. **Family:** Lily. **Comments:** The flowers, sometimes greenish, are in huge clusters. This plant is poisonous to grazing animals. Green wood lily, *V. viride,* has green flowers in drooping clusters and ovate leaves; fringed corn lily, *V. insolitum,* has white flowers with fringed petal-like parts and elliptic leaves.

Bear Grass, *Xerophyllum tenax*

Flowers: In dense terminal clusters (racemes) up to 1½' long, on white stalks. **Petal-like Parts:** 6, separated, veined, about ⅜" long. **Stems:** Robust, up to 6' tall. **Leaves:** Simple; the numerous basal leaves are in a dense tuft, very long and narrow, without teeth, hard, dry, to 3' long. **Season:** May–Aug. **Habitat:** Dry ridges, open woods. **Range** (*see map*): Areas 8–10, C. **Family:** Lily. **Comments:** The fibers of the leaves were used by Indians for making garments. The rootstocks can be eaten when roasted. Turkey beard, *X. asphodeloides,* has leaves minutely toothed along the edges.

White Camas, *Zigadenus elegans*

Flowers: Many, in a long cluster (raceme). **Petal-like Parts:** 6, white, separated, up to ½" long, with a 2-lobed gland. **Stems:** Upright, up to 2½' tall. **Leaves:** Alternate, simple, crowded toward the base of the plant, linear; up to 1½' long and ½" wide. **Season:** June–Sept. **Habitat:** Wet ledges in mountains. **Range** (*see map*): Areas 3–9, A–F. **Family:** Lily. **Comments:** The petal-like parts are sometimes marked with purple or brown. Crow poison, *Z. densus,* has flowers in a raceme and petal-like parts ¼" long; smooth camas, *Z. glaberrimus,* has flowers in a different type of cluster (a panicle) and petal-like parts at least ½" long; white camas, *V. glaucus,* also has flowers in a panicle and petal-like parts less than ½" long; veiny camas, *Z. venenosus,* has flowers in a raceme, the leaves folded lengthwise, and petal-like parts less than ½" long.

▲ False Solomon's Seal
6 separated petal-like parts.

Corn Lily ▶
6 separated petal-like parts.

▼ Bear Grass
6 separated petal-like parts.

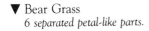

▼ White Camas
6 separated petal-like parts.

RADIAL SYMMETRY

Spider Lily, *Hymenocallis occidentalis*

Flowers: Usually 3–6 in a cluster (umbel). **Petal-like Parts:** 6, very narrow and up to 2″ long, wide-spreading, with a membranous petal-like funnel at the base of each flower. **Stems:** Up to 2′ tall, smooth, bearing only the flowers. **Leaves:** All basal, strap-shaped, smooth, up to 1½′ long, nearly 2″ wide. **Season:** April–June. **Habitat:** Swamps, wet ditches, low woods. **Range** (*see map*): Areas 2 and 3. **Family:** Lily. **Comments:** The long-spreading slender petal-like parts give rise to the common name.

White Hyacinth, *Triteleia hyacinthina*

Flowers: About 10–40 in a cluster (umbel), each flower up to ½″ across on a stalk up to 2″ long. **Petal-like Parts:** 6, united near the base, each with a green vein. **Stems:** Upright, smooth, up to 2½′ tall. **Leaves:** Few, smooth, long and narrow, up to 18″ long. **Season:** March–Aug. **Habitat:** Low, moist areas. **Range** (*see map*): Areas 8–10, C. **Family:** Lily. **Comments:** The cup-shaped flowers are unusual for the genus *Triteleia.* Grass nut, *T. laxa,* of California has violet-purple flowers.

Zephyr Lily, *Zephyranthes atamasco*

Flowers: Solitary, up to 4″ long. **Petal-like Parts:** 6, united at the base. **Stems:** Upright, smooth, to nearly 1′ tall. **Leaves:** All basal, long and slender, up to 18″ long, less than ½″ wide. **Season:** March–June. **Habitat:** Low woods, wet meadows. **Range** (*see map*): Areas 1 and 2. **Family:** Lily. **Comments:** This species is distinguished from other zephyr lilies by its white flowers. Simpson's zephr lily, *Z. simpsonii,* has pinkish flowers less than 3″ long; narrow-leaved rain lily, *Z. longifolia,* has pink-tinged flowers and thread-like leaves about ⅛″ wide; yellow rain lily, *Z. pulchella,* has bright yellow flowers about 1″ long and broader leaves.

Lizard's Tail, *Saururus cernuus*

Flowers: Crowded into an elongated, arched spike up to 6″ long. **Petals:** None. **Stems:** Branched, smooth, up to 3′ tall. **Leaves:** Alternate, simple, ovate, heart-shaped at the base, without teeth; smooth, up to 6″ long. **Season:** June–Aug. **Habitat:** Swamps and marshes. **Range** (*see map*): Areas 1–3, 5, 6, E. **Family:** Lizard's tail. **Comments:** The color of the flowers is due to the numerous white stamens. The underground stem (rhizome) is fragrant. This is the only member of its genus in North America.

▲ Spider Lily
  6 united petal-like parts.

▲ White Hyacinth
  6 united petal-like parts.

Zephyr Lily ▲
*6 united
petal-like parts.*

Lizard's Tail ▶
No petals.

RADIAL SYMMETRY

Water Cress, *Nasturtium officinale*

Flowers: Several, in elongated terminal clusters (racemes), each flower up to ¼″ across. **Petals:** 4, separated. **Stems:** Floating in water or lying flat on muddy soil, smooth. **Leaves:** Alternate, pinnately compound, with 3–9 leaflets; the leaflets are smooth, round-tipped, toothed; the terminal leaflet is larger than the others. **Season:** March–Oct. **Habitat:** Clear water, often springs. **Range** (*see map*): Areas 1–10. **Family:** Mustard. **Comments:** This species may be used in salads to provide a mild peppery taste. Small water cress, *N. microphyllum*, is similar except for its much smaller leaflets.

Common Toothwort, *Dentaria laciniata*

Flowers: Several, in terminal clusters (racemes), each flower up to ¾″ long. **Petals:** 4, separated, narrow. **Stems:** Upright, unbranched, usually somewhat hairy above, up to 1′ tall. **Leaves:** Basal as well as 3 stem leaves in a whorl below the flowers, palmately compound with coarsely toothed leaflets, smooth. **Season:** March–May. **Habitat:** Rich, shaded woods. **Range** (*see map*): Areas 1–6, E. **Family:** Mustard. **Comments:** The petals may be pale lavender or pink. The roots taste something like radishes. Large toothwort, *D. maxima*, has alternate leaves on the stem; smooth toothwort, *D. heterophylla*, has completely smooth stems and stalked leaflets; opposite-leaved toothwort, *D. diphylla*, has a pair of opposite, compound leaves below the flowers.

Bunchberry, *Cornus canadensis*

Flowers: Several, grouped into a compact cluster surrounded by 4 conspicuous, white leaf-like structures (bracts); bracts are ovate, up to ¾″ long. **Stems:** Upright, smooth, up to 8″ tall. **Leaves:** Opposite, simple, lanceolate to obovate, pointed at the tip; smooth, up to 3″ long, the veins arising a short distance above the base. **Season:** June–Aug. **Habitat:** Bogs, moist woods. **Range** (*see map*): All areas except 2 and 6. **Family:** Dogwood. **Comments:** This tiny species is related to the flowering dogwood and the Pacific dogwood, both trees with showy bracts. Boreal dogwood, *C. suecica*, is a low-growing herb with large bracts but fewer veins in the leaf, all of which arise from the base.

Buttonweed, *Diodia virginiana*

Flowers: Solitary, in the leaf axils, up to ½″ long, without a stalk. **Petals:** 4, united below into a slender tube. **Stems:** Lying flat on the ground, hairy. **Leaves:** Opposite, simple, elliptic to lanceolate, without teeth; hairy, up to 2½″ long. **Season:** June–Aug. **Habitat:** Wet soil. **Range** (*see map*): Areas 1–3, 6. **Family:** Madder. **Comments:** The presence of thread-like bristles (stipules) at the base of each leaf is characteristic of the buttonweeds. Rough buttonweed, *D. teres*, is a plant of dry soil and usually has pink flowers.

▲ Water Cress
4 separated petals.

▲ Common Toothwort
4 separated petals.

▲ Bunchberry
4 separated petals.

▲ Buttonweed
4 united petals.

RADIAL SYMMETRY

Water Hemlock, *Cicuta maculata*

Flowers: Many, in several terminal clusters (umbels). **Petals:** 5, separated. **Stems:** Upright, branched, smooth, up to 8′ tall. **Leaves:** Alternate, twice pinnately compound; the leaflets are coarsely toothed, smooth. **Season:** May–Sept. **Habitat:** Marshes, wet prairies, moist woods, wet ditches. **Range** (*see map*): All areas except 10 and A. **Family:** Carrot. **Comments:** All parts of this plant are poisonous. Western water hemlock, *C. douglasii*, is very similar, but has fruit with red-brown markings; cowbane, *C. mexicana*, has notched fruits; bulbous water hemlock, *C. bulbifera*, is a smaller plant up to 3′ tall with bulbs in the leaf axils; poison hemlock, *Conium maculatum*, has much more deeply divided leaves.

Queen Anne's Lace (Wild Carrot), *Daucus carota*

Flowers: Many, in several terminal clusters (umbels), each flower up to ⅛″ across. **Petals:** 5, separated. **Stems:** Upright, branched, hairy, up to 4′ tall. **Leaves:** Alternate, twice pinnately compound; the leaflets are lobed or toothed, hairy. **Season:** June–Sept. **Habitat:** Roadsides, fields. **Range** (*see map*): Areas 1–10, C–F. **Family:** Carrot. **Comments:** This is the same species as the cultivated carrot. The innermost flower of the umbel is often purplish. Dwarf carrot, *D. pusillus*, is less than 3′ tall and has smaller umbels; sweet cicely, *Osmorhiza longistylis*, is a woodland species with broad leaflets and the odor of licorice.

Rattlesnake Master, *Eryngium yuccifolium*

Flowers: Crowded into a spherical head nearly 1″ in diameter. **Petals:** 5, separated. **Stems:** Upright, usually unbranched, smooth, up to 5′ tall. **Leaves:** Alternate, simple, linear, with spiny teeth along the edges; up to 2½′ long. **Season:** July–Sept. **Habitat:** Prairies, open woods. **Range** (*see map*): Areas 1–3, 5, 6. **Family:** Carrot. **Comments:** This species does not resemble other members of the carrot family since the flowers do not have stalks, resulting in a spherical head rather than an umbel. Leavenworth eryngo, *E. leavenworthii*, has leaves up to 3″ long and purple-red flowering heads about 1½″ long; creeping eryngo, *E. prostratum*, is a dwarf, creeping plant with small, elongated, purple heads.

Cow Parsnip, *Heracleum lanatum*

Flowers: Tiny and formed into huge clusters (umbels) nearly 1′ across. **Petals:** 5, separated. **Stems:** Stout, hairy, up to 10′ tall. **Leaves:** Alternate, compound, usually 3-parted or the lower merely lobed; the leaflets are hairy, toothed and lobed, up to 6″ across. **Season:** June–Aug. **Habitat:** Moist soil in woods and fields. **Range** (*see map*): All areas except 6. **Family:** Carrot. **Comments:** This species is poisonous to cattle. It is named for the Greek hero Hercules, who supposedly found medicinal qualities in parts of the plant. Other similar members of the carrot family include water parsnip, *Sium suave*, with lower leaves more deeply divided than the upper leaves; and cowherb, *Oxypolis rigidior*, with large leaflets with few or no teeth.

▲ Water Hemlock
  5 separated petals.
  Clusters: umbels.

▲ Queen Anne's Lace
  5 separated petals. Clusters: umbels.

▲ Rattlesnake Master
  5 separated petals.
  Clusters: umbels.

▲ Cow Parsnip
  5 separated petals. Clusters: umbels.

RADIAL SYMMETRY

Lovage, *Ligusticum porteri*

Flowers: Small, arranged in flat-topped clusters (umbels). **Petals:** 5, separated. **Stems:** Robust, branched, smooth or hairy, up to 3′ tall. **Leaves:** Alternate, twice pinnately compound; the leaflets are ovate, up to 2″ long. **Season:** June–Aug. **Habitat:** Wet soil, often in mountain woods. **Range** (*see map*): Areas 7–9. **Family:** Carrot. **Comments:** The flowers are sometimes pinkish. Eastern lovage, *L. canadense*, is similar but has fewer, larger-toothed leaflets up to 3½″ long. Chervil, *Chaerophyllum procumbens*, is a low-growing plant with hairy, much divided, fern-like leaves that can be used in salads.

Hedge Parsley, *Torilis japonica*

Flowers: Several, crowded into many clusters (umbels), each flower about ⅙″ long. **Petals:** 5, separated. **Stems:** Upright, branched, hairy, up to 3′ tall. **Leaves:** Alternate, much divided, with the segments toothed or lobed; hairy. **Season:** July–Sept. **Habitat:** Along roads, in fields. **Range** (*see map*): Areas 1–3, 5, 9, 10, E. **Family:** Carrot. **Comments:** This hedge parsley has its flower clusters on stalks up to 6″ long. The similar jointed parsley, *T. nodosa*, has flower clusters on stalks only ½″ long.

Spring Beauty, *Claytonia virginica*

Flowers: Several, in terminal clusters (racemes), each flower up to 1″ across. **Petals:** 5, white, often with pink striations. **Stems:** Weak, upright, smooth, up to 6″ tall. **Leaves:** Opposite, simple, elongated and narrow, without teeth; smooth, up to 6″ long and ½″ wide. **Season:** March–July. **Habitat:** Rich, shaded woods. **Range** (*see map*): Areas 1–3, 5, 6, E. **Family:** Portulaca. **Comments:** The roots taste something like chestnuts when roasted. Lance-leaved spring beauty, *C. lanceolata*, has pink or white flowers and lanceolate to ovate leaves up to 3″ long; large-rooted spring beauty, *C. megarhiza*, has large purple-red taproots and white or pink flowers.

Galax, *Galax aphylla*

Flowers: Several, crowded into a slender terminal cluster (raceme), each flower up to ¼″ long. **Petals:** 5, separated. **Stems:** Leafless, upright, smooth, up to 15″ tall. **Leaves:** All basal, simple, ovate, heart-shaped at base, toothed; evergreen, smooth, up to 6″ long, usually with much shorter stalks. **Season:** June–July. **Habitat:** Mountain woods. **Range** (*see map*): Areas 1 and 2. **Family:** Diapensia. **Comments:** The leaves of this mountain species are used for Christmas decorations.

▲ Lovage
   5 separated petals. Clusters: umbels.

▼ Hedge Parsley
   5 separated petals. Clusters: umbels.

▼ Spring Beauty
   5 separated petals. 6 stamens.

▲ Galax
   5 separated petals. Basal leaves.

RADIAL SYMMETRY

Smooth Woodland Star, *Lithophragma glabra*

Flowers: 5–10 in a terminal cluster (raceme). **Petals:** 5, separated, 3-lobed at tip. **Stems:** Slender, smooth, up to 18″ tall. **Leaves:** Mostly basal, smooth, usually round-lobed. **Season:** March–May. **Habitat:** Moist woods. **Range** (*see map*): Areas 4, 8–10. **Family:** Saxifrage. **Comments:** Other species of *Lithophragma* include hairy woodland star, *L. affine*, with hairy stems and leaves; prairie star, *L. parviflorum*, with flowers ¼″ across and usually 5-lobed leaves; and slender prairie star, *L. tenellum*, with flowers 1″ across.

Bouncing Bet, *Saponaria officinalis*

Flowers: Several, in clusters arising from the upper leaf axils, fragrant, each flower up to 1½″ long. **Petals:** 5, separated, usually notched at the tip. **Stems:** Upright, branched or unbranched, smooth, up to 2′ tall. **Leaves:** Opposite, simple, elliptic, without teeth; usually smooth, up to 4″ long. **Season:** May–Sept. **Habitat:** Roadsides, fields, along railroads. **Range** (*see map*): All areas except A and B. **Family:** Pink. **Comments:** The petals may be pinkish. Double-flowered forms with extra petals sometimes occur. Cowherb, *Vaccaria pyramidata*, is similar but is an annual with pink flowers and winged sepals.

Bladder Catchfly, *Silene cucubalus*

Flowers: In terminal clusters, each flower up to ¾″ across. **Petals:** 5, separated, deeply notched at tip. **Stems:** Upright, branched, smooth, up to 1½′ tall. **Leaves:** Opposite, simple, oblong to broadly lanceolate, without teeth; smooth, up to 4″ long. **Season:** May–Aug. **Habitat:** Fields, roadsides. **Range** (*see map*): All areas except 6, 7, B. **Family:** Pink. **Comments:** The swollen bladdery fruits and the deeply notched petals help differentiate this species. Nodding catchfly, *S. noctiflora*, is similar but has hairy stems; European catchfly, *S. gallica*, has narrower leaves and unnotched petals; Menzies' catchfly, *S. menziesii*, a matted plant about 8″ tall, has smaller flowers with 2- or 4-lobed petals; sleepy catchfly, *S. antirrhina*, is a slender species with flowers less than ½″ long. White campion, *Lychnis alba*, is very similar to the bladder catchfly but has the stamens and pistils in separate flowers.

Pokeweed, *Phytolacca americana*

Flowers: Several, in terminal clusters (racemes), each flower up to ⅓″ across. **Petals:** None, but the 5 sepals are white and petal-like. **Stems:** Robust, branched above, smooth, up to 10′ tall. **Leaves:** Alternate, simple, lanceolate to ovate, without teeth; smooth, up to 10″ long. **Season:** July–Oct. **Habitat:** Woods, fields, roadsides. **Range** (*see map*): Areas 2, 6, 7. **Family:** Pokeweed. **Comments:** The flowers may have a pinkish tinge. The young shoots are sometimes eaten as greens, but they become poisonous as they mature and turn purple. Pigeon-berry, *Rivina humilis*, is only about 3′ tall and has only 4 stamens in each flower rather than 10.

◀ Smooth Woodland Star
  5 separated petals.
  10 stamens.

▲ Bouncing Bet
  5 separated petals.
  10 stamens.

◀ Bladder Catchfly
  5 separated petals.
  10 stamens.

▼ Pokeweed
  5 separated petal-like
  parts. 10 stamens.

RADIAL SYMMETRY

Flowering Spurge, *Euphorbia corollata*

Flowers: Several, in stalked clusters, each flower less than ½″ across.
Petal-like Parts: 5, separated, about ⅕″ long. **Stems:** Upright, branched,
smooth or hairy, up to 3′ tall. **Leaves:** Alternate, simple, linear to elliptic,
without teeth; smooth or hairy, up to 2½″ long. **Season:** June–Oct.
Habitat: Woods, prairies, fields. **Range** (*see map*): Areas 1–6, E. **Family:**
Spurge. **Comments:** The 5 white petal-like parts, alternate leaves, and
milky sap distinguish this species. Common spurge, *E. hexagona*, has
opposite leaves and even smaller flowers.

Snow-on-the-mountain, *Euphorbia marginata*

Flowers: Several small flowers in terminal clusters, surrounded from below
by oblong leaf-like structures (bracts) with white borders. **Petal-like Parts:**
5, white. **Stems:** Upright, hairy, up to 2½′ tall. **Leaves:** Alternate,
simple, ovate to elliptic, without teeth; smooth or hairy, up to 4″ long,
without stalks. **Season:** June–Oct. **Habitat:** Prairies, plains. **Range** (*see
map*): Areas 1–7, D, E. **Family:** Spurge. **Comments:** This species is
conspicuous because of its white-bordered bracts beneath the flower clusters.
It is often grown in gardens. The variegated spurge, *E. bicolor*, has linear
leaves beneath the cluster of flowers.

Sand Lily, *Mentzelia decapetala*

Flowers: 1 to a few in a terminal cluster, each flower up to 3″ long.
Petals: 10, white, separated. **Stems:** Upright, stout, rough and hairy,
yellowish, up to 3′ tall. **Leaves:** Alternate, simple, sharply toothed or
lobed, lanceolate; hairy, up to 6″ long. **Season:** July–Sept. **Habitat:**
Prairies, roadsides, open areas. **Range** (*see map*): Areas 3–9, C, D. **Family:**
Stick-leaf. **Comments:** The flowers usually open after sunset. Similar
species are the white stick-leaf, *M. nuda*, with white flowers about 2″ long;
white-stemmed stick-leaf, *M. albescens*, with yellow petals ½″ long; blazing
star, *M. multiflora*, with yellow petals nearly 1″ long; Reverchon's blazing
star, *M. reverchonii*, with yellow petals 1½″ long.

Mayapple, *Podophyllum peltatum*

Flowers: Solitary, in the axils of paired leaves, up to 2″ across. **Petals:** 6
(occasionally more), separated. **Stems:** Upright, smooth, up to 2′ tall.
Leaves: 1 or 2 per plant, deeply divided into 5–9 parts; umbrella-like,
attached at the center to the stalk; usually smooth, up to 14″ across.
Season: April–June. **Habitat:** Woods. **Range** (*see map*) Areas 1–5, D–
F. **Family:** Barberry. **Comments:** The underground stem is poisonous.
The fruit may be eaten raw, made into jam, or made into a drink. A
similar species is twinleaf, *Jeffersonia diphylla*, which has 2-lobed leaves at
the base of the plant and smaller flowers with 8 petals.

▲ Flowering Spurge
5 separated petal-like parts.
Milky sap.

Snow-on-the-mountain ▶
5 separated petal-like parts.
Milky sap.

▲ Sand Lily
10 separated petals.
10–18 stamens.

▲ Mayapple
6–10 separated petals.
10–18 stamens.

RADIAL SYMMETRY

Bloodroot, *Sanguinaria canadensis*

Flowers: Solitary on a leafless stalk, up to 1½″ across. **Petals:** 8–15, white, up to 1″ long, lasting only one day. **Stems:** Underground, containing red sap. **Leaves:** All at the base of the plant, about as wide as they are long, palmately lobed; smooth, up to 3″ across. **Season:** Feb–May. **Habitat:** Rich, moist woods. **Range** (*see map*): Areas 1–6, D–F. **Family:** Poppy. **Comments:** The underground stem has poisonous properties. The red sap can stain the skin. This is the only species of the genus in North America.

Water Lily, *Nymphaea odorata*

Flowers: Solitary, fragrant, up to 6″ across. **Petals:** Numerous, separated, tapering to the tip. **Leaves:** Round, floating in water, smooth, usually purple on the lower surface, up to 10″ across. **Season:** June–Sept. **Habitat:** In ponds, lakes, or quiet streams. **Range** (*see map*): Areas 1–3, 5–9, D–F. **Family:** Water Lily. **Comments:** The flowers of this lovely aquatic open in the morning. Another water lily, *N. tuberosa*, has odorless flowers; blue water lily, *N. elegans*, has flowers with 6–10 blue or violet petals.

White Prickly Poppy, *Argemone polyanthemos*

Flowers: Up to 4½″ across, with 1–2 leaf-like structures (bracts) close by. **Petals:** 4, separated. **Stems:** Upright, prickly, to 5′ tall. **Leaves:** Alternate, lobed, prickly at least on the veins. **Season:** April–Nov. **Habitat:** Prairies, mesas, roadsides, fields, pastures. **Range** (*see map*): Areas 3–9. **Family:** Poppy. **Comments:** The 2 inner petals are narrower than the 2 outer ones. The numerous yellow stamens provide a beautiful contrast to the white petals. Yellow prickly poppy, *A. mexicana*, has flowers 3″ across, yellow petals, and fewer stamens.

Liverleaf, *Hepatica nobilis*

Flowers: Solitary, up to 1″ across, surrounded from below by 3 leaf-like structures (bracts), on hairy stalks up to 8″ long. **Petals:** None, but the 5–9 sepals are petal-like. **Stems:** Underground, horizontal. **Leaves:** All basal, 3-lobed, leathery, more or less evergreen, hairy, up to 2½″ across. **Season:** Feb–March. **Habitat:** Rich woods. **Range** (*see map*): Areas 1–3, D–F. **Family:** Buttercup. **Comments:** The lobes of the leaves may be pointed or rounded at the tip.

▲ Water Lily
Many separated petals. Many stamens.

▲ Bloodroot
8–15 separated petals.
Many stamens.

White Prickly Poppy ▶
4 separated petals. Many stamens.

▼ Liverleaf
5–9 petal-like parts. Many stamens.

RADIAL SYMMETRY

Dogbane, *Apocynum cannabinum*

Flowers: Several in terminal and axillary clusters, about ⅙″ long. **Petals:** 5, united below. **Stems:** Erect, branched, usually smooth, up to 5′ tall, with milky sap. **Leaves:** Opposite, simple, oblong to lanceolate-ovate, pointed at the tip, without teeth; smooth or sometimes hairy, with milky sap, up to 2½″ across, borne on short stalks. **Season:** May–Aug. **Habitat:** Prairies, fields, woods. **Range** (*see map*): All areas except A, B, and D. **Family:** Dogbane. **Comments:** The milky sap is poisonous. Dogbanes differ from milkweeds by their simpler flower structures and their fruits that are borne in pairs, rather than singly. Spreading dogbane, *A. androsaemifolium*, has larger flowers that are usually pink; intermediate dogbane, *A. medium*, has white flowers about ¼″ long; Siberian dogbane, *A. sibiricum*, has leaves without stalks.

Wild Sweet Potato Vine, *Ipomoea pandurata*

Flowers: 1–7 in terminal clusters, each flower up to 4″ long. **Petals:** 5, white with a purple base, united into a funnel. **Stems:** Trailing or twining, smooth, up to 15′ long. **Leaves:** Alternate, simple, ovate, without teeth; smooth, up to 6″ long. **Season:** June–Sept. **Habitat:** Woods, fields. **Range** (*see map*): Areas 1–3, 5, 6, E. **Family:** Morning glory. **Comments:** A similar twining plant with large white flowers is the hedge bindweed, *Calystegia sepium*, but its petals are not purple at the base.

Morning-glory Bindweed, *Heliotropium convolvulaceum*

Flowers: Funnel-shaped, white with a yellow center, about 1″ across. **Petals:** United below into a tube ½″ long. **Stems:** Upright, hairy, up to 18″ tall. **Leaves:** Alternate, simple, lanceolate to ovate, without teeth; hairy, up to 2″ long, about ¾″ wide. **Season:** June–Oct. **Habitat:** Sandy soil. **Range** (*see map*): Areas 2, 5–8, 10. **Family:** Forget-me-not. **Comments:** The fragrant flowers resemble morning glories. Seaside heliotrope, *H. curassavicum*, has smooth stems and leaves, is somewhat fleshy, and has white flowers about ⅙″ long; slender heliotrope, *H. tenellum*, has tiny white flowers with a yellow center and leaves less than ¼″ wide.

White Phlox, *Phlox diffusa*

Flowers: Few, at the tips of the branches, up to ⅔″ wide. **Petals:** United below into a slender tube up to ⅔″ long. **Stems:** Sprawling, up to 10″ long, smooth or sparsely hairy. **Leaves:** Opposite, simple, nearly needle-like, about ½″ long. **Season:** May–Aug. **Habitat:** Open areas. **Range** (*see map*): Areas 7, 9, 10, C. **Family:** Phlox. **Comments:** The white flowers and needle-like leaves readily distinguish this species. Cleft phlox, *P. bifida*, is a creeping plant with very narrow leaves and pale lavender flowers with notched petals.

◀ Dogbane
5 united petals. 5 stamens.

▼ Morning-glory Bindweed
5 united petals. 5 stamens.

▼ Wild Sweet Potato Vine
5 united petals. 5 stamens.

▼ White Phlox
5 united petals. 5 stamens.

RADIAL SYMMETRY

Fendler's Waterleaf, *Hydrophyllum fendleri*

Flowers: Several, crowded into a spherical head. **Petals:** About ½" long, united about halfway from the base. **Stems:** Erect, up to 2′ tall, hairy. **Leaves:** Alternate, deeply divided into 7–13 sharply toothed segments; up to 12" long. **Season:** May–Aug. **Habitat:** In woods and along streams. **Range** (*see map*): Areas 7–10, C. **Family:** Waterleaf. **Comments:** The combination of white flowers in a head and 7–13 leaflets distinguishes this species. Pacific waterleaf, *H. tenuipes,* has white flowers in a head but only 5 leaflets; capitate waterleaf, *H. capitatum,* has white or bluish flowers in a head and 5–7 sparsely toothed leaflets.

Variable Phacelia, *Phacelia heterophylla*

Flowers: Crowded into short, curved clusters. **Petals:** United below, up to ⅓" long, sometimes varying to pink or pale purple. **Stems:** Erect, up to 2′ tall, hairy. **Leaves:** Basal and alternate; extremely variable, some of them unlobed, others with 3 or 5 lobes, never toothed; hairy, up to 4" long. **Season:** May–July. **Habitat:** Rocky, wooded areas. **Range** (*see map*): Areas 1, 3, 7–10. **Family:** Waterleaf. **Comments:** This species is characterized by having both lobed and unlobed toothless leaves. *Phacelia* has dozens of species in the western U.S.A. and a few in the East; many are blue-flowered. Other white-flowered species include the stinging phacelia, *P. malvifolia,* with maple-shaped leaves; tall phacelia, *P. procera,* with sharp-pointed leaf lobes; and silvery phacelia, *P. hastata,* with silvery gray, lanceolate leaves.

Jimson-weed, *Datura stramonium*

Flowers: Few, large, up to nearly 4" long, about 2" wide, sometimes with a purple center. **Petals:** United below into a long tube. **Stems:** Erect, branched, up to 5′ tall, smooth or nearly so. **Leaves:** Alternate, simple, ovate to elliptic, coarsely toothed or lobed; smooth or nearly so, up to 8" long. **Season:** April–Nov. **Habitat:** Fields, roadsides. **Range** (*see map*): All areas except A and B. **Family:** Nightshade. **Comments:** This plant was introduced by early settlers and was originally called Jamestown weed. The seeds are poisonous. Other daturas, with flowers usually about 6" long, are the Indian apple, *D. innoxia,* with nearly smooth leaves; and Wright's datura, *D. wrightii,* with velvety leaves.

Horse Nettle, *Solanum carolinense*

Flowers: Few, in terminal clusters, up to ¾" across. **Petals:** Spreading, united for about half their length. **Stems:** Erect, branched, hairy and often with short yellow prickles, to 3′ tall. **Leaves:** Alternate, simple, oblong to ovate, with a few coarse teeth or lobes; hairy, often prickly on the veins, up to 6" long. **Season:** June–Oct. **Habitat:** Open areas. **Range** (*see map*): Areas 1–8, D, E. **Family:** Nightshade. **Comments:** The yellow berry is poisonous. Black nightshade, *S. americanum,* is a smooth species with small white flowers and poisonous black berries; cutleaf nightshade, *S. triflorum,* is a hairy, nonprickly species with small white flowers.

Fendler's Waterleaf ▶
5 united petals. 5 stamens.

▼ Variable Phacelia
5 united petals. 5 stamens.

▼ Jimson-weed
5 united petals. 5 stamens.

▲ Horse Nettle
5 united petals. 5 stamens.

RADIAL SYMMETRY

Shooting Star, *Dodecatheon meadia*

Flowers: Few to several in terminal clusters (umbels), each flower up to 1⅓″ long. **Petals:** 5, turned backward, united at the base. **Stems:** All underground. **Leaves:** Basal, oblong to oblanceolate; smooth, up to 12″ long and 4″ wide. **Season:** April–June. **Habitat:** Woods, prairies. **Range** (*see map*): Areas 1–3, 5, 6. **Family:** Primrose. **Comments:** The turned-back petals and sharply pointed stamens account for the common name. Several other shooting stars, including some mountain species found above the tree line, occur in North America: western shooting star, *D. pulchellum*, has lavender to magenta petals; alpine shooting star, *D. alpinum*, has only 4 pink petals.

Indian Pipe, *Monotropa uniflora*

Flowers: Solitary, hanging downward, about ½″ long. **Petals:** United at base. **Stems:** Upright, waxy, white, up to 8″ tall. **Leaves:** Reduced to colorless scales. **Season:** June–Oct. **Habitat:** Woods, in leaf mold. **Range** (*see map*): All areas except 7, 8, and B. **Family:** Indian Pipe. **Comments:** Indian pipe is parasitic on soil fungi. The plants turn black when dry. A second *Monotropa* is called pinesap, *M. hypopithys*; it has more than one flower per stem.

Bindweed, *Convolvulus arvensis*

Flowers: 1–3 in the leaf axils, up to 1″ across. **Petals:** Spreading, united below into an elongated tube. **Stems:** Creeping on ground, up to 3′ long, smooth or hairy. **Leaves:** Alternate, simple, some arrowhead-shaped, without teeth; smooth, up to 2″ long. **Season:** May–Oct. **Habitat:** Open areas. **Range** (*see map*): All areas except A and B. **Family:** Morning glory. **Comments:** Large-flowered bindweeds, with flowers up to 3″ long, include hedge bindweed, *Calystegia sepium*, with twining stems; and upright bindweed, *Calystegia spithamaea*, with erect stems.

BILATERAL SYMMETRY

Slender Mountain Mint, *Pycnanthemum tenuifolium*

Flowers: Several, in dense terminal clusters, the clusters up to ½″ across. **Petals:** Purple-speckled, united below. **Stems:** Upright, branched, usually smooth, to 2′ tall. **Leaves:** Opposite, simple, very narrow and elongated, without teeth; smooth or slightly hairy, about ⅛″ wide. **Season:** June–Sept. **Habitat:** Fields, prairies, dry woods. **Range** (*see map*): Areas 1–3, 5, 6, E. **Family:** Mint. **Comments:** This species has the narrowest leaves of any mountain mint. Other common species include white mountain mint, *P. albescens*, with the uppermost leaves conspicuously hairy-white; Virginia mountain mint, *P. virginianum*, with all leaves green and at least ⅙″ wide, and hairy mountain mint, *P. pilosum*, with small flower heads surrounded from below by velvety leaves.

▲ Shooting Star
  5 united petals, turned backward. 5 stamens.

▼ Indian Pipe
  5 united petals.
  8 or 10 stamens. Plants not green.

▼ Bindweed
  United petals.
  Plants creeping.

▼ Slender Mountain Mint
  United petals.

BILATERAL SYMMETRY

White Turtlehead, *Chelone glabra*

Flowers: Several, in terminal spikes, each flower up to 1½" long. **Petals:** 2-lipped, the mouth barely open. **Stems:** Upright, sometimes branched, up to 4½' tall, smooth. **Leaves:** Opposite, simple, linear to ovate-lanceolate, toothed; smooth, up to 6" long. **Season:** July–Sept. **Habitat:** Low woods. **Range** (*see map*): Areas 1–3, E, F. **Family:** Snapdragon. **Comments:** Some specimens have purple-tinted petals. Another showy turtlehead is the purple turtlehead, *C. obliqua,* with purple petals.

Squirrel-corn, *Dicentra canadensis*

Flowers: Several, in clusters (racemes) on a leafless stalk, each flower up to ⅔" long, nodding, fragrant. **Petals:** 4, in 2 pairs, with rounded spurs at the base. **Leaves:** All basal, delicately divided and fern-like, smooth. **Season:** March–May. **Habitat:** Rich woods. **Range** (*see map*): Areas 1–3, E. **Family:** Poppy. **Comments:** The underground tubers resemble yellow kernels of corn. The eastern wild bleeding heart, *D. eximia* (map areas 1 and 2), and the western wild bleeding heart, *D. formosa* (map areas 9, 10, C) are similar but have pink to rose-purple flowers.

Steer's Head, *Dicentra uniflora*

Flowers: Solitary, on a slender, leafless stalk, the flower up to ⅔" long. **Petals:** 4, in 2 pairs, the outer 2 curving backwards to form "horns." **Leaves:** All basal, smooth, pinnately divided. **Season:** Feb–June. **Habitat:** Woods and open areas. **Range** (*see map*): Areas 8–10, C. **Family:** Poppy. **Comments:** The flowers are sometimes pink. The resemblance of the flower to a steer's head is remarkable.

Dutchman's Breeches, *Dicentra cucullaria*

Flowers: Several, in clusters (racemes) on a leafless stalk up to 10" long, each flower up to ⅔" long, up to ¾" wide, nodding. **Petals:** 4, in 2 pairs, white except for the yellow tip, spreading above, with pointed spurs at the base. **Leaves:** All basal, very delicately divided, fern-like; pale on the lower surface, smooth. **Season:** March–May. **Habitat:** Rich woods. **Range** (*see map*): Areas 1–6, 9, E, F. **Family:** Poppy. **Comments:** This attractive wildflower is suitable for shaded wildflower gardens. It contains a chemical poisonous to cattle.

▲ White Turtlehead
United petals.

▼ Squirrel-corn
United petals.

◀ Steer's Head
United petals.

▼ Dutchman's Breeches
United petals.

BILATERAL SYMMETRY

White Prairie Clover, *Dalea candida*

Flowers: Crowded into terminal spikes up to 3½" long. **Petals:** 5, separated, unequal in size. **Stems:** Upright, smooth, up to 2' tall. **Leaves:** Alternate, pinnately compound, with 5–9 smooth, toothless leaflets. **Season:** June–Aug. **Habitat:** Prairies, dry woods. **Range** (*see map*): All areas except 10, A, B, F. **Family:** Pea. **Comments:** Similar species are the round-headed prairie clover, *D. multiflora*, with white, nearly spherical flower heads; and purple prairie clover, *D. purpurea*, with elongated, purple flower spikes.

White Clover, *Trifolium repens*

Flowers: Many, crowded into spherical heads up to 1" across, each flower less than ½" long. **Petals:** Unlike in size and shape. **Stems:** Creeping on the ground, with the tips turned upward, smooth or slightly hairy, up to 1' long. **Leaves:** Alternate, divided into 3 leaflets; the leaflets are obovate, rounded or shallowly notched at the tip, with small teeth, smooth, up to ¾" long. **Season:** May–Oct. **Habitat:** Fields, lawns, roadsides. **Range** (*see map*): All areas. **Family:** Pea. **Comments:** This is an excellent plant to control soil erosion because the stems root tenaciously into the soil. Alsike clover, *T. hybridum*, is very similar but has pinkish flowers.

White Violet, *Viola striata*

Flowers: Solitary, arising from the leaf axils, up to 1¼" long. **Petals:** 5, white, with purple lines; one petal has a short, blunt spur. **Stems:** Erect, smooth, up to 10" long. **Leaves:** Alternate, simple, nearly round to ovate, round-toothed; smooth, up to 1½" long. The small leaf-like structures (stipules) at the base of the leaf stalks are jagged-toothed. **Season:** April–June. **Habitat:** Low woods. **Range** (*see map*): 1–3, 5, 6, E. **Family:** Violet. **Comments:** White-flowered violets with above-ground stems and leaf-like stipules that are not jagged-toothed include Canada violet, *V. canadensis*, with smooth leaves; and wrinkled violet, *V. rugulosa*, with hairy leaves. White-flowered violets with all stems underground include sweet white violet, *V. blanda*, with hairy leaves heart-shaped at the base; wild white violet, *V. pallens*, with smooth leaves heart-shaped at the base.

Bog Rein Orchid, *Platanthera dilatata*

Flowers: Several, in an elongated terminal cluster, very fragrant. **Petals and Sepals:** Some segments forming a hood about ¼" long, the lip petal somewhat swollen. **Stems:** Upright, up to 4½' tall. **Leaves:** Lanceolate, up to 1' long. **Season:** June–Sept. **Habitat:** Wet woods, bogs, meadows. **Range** (*see map*): All areas except 2 and 6. **Family:** Orchid. **Comments:** The flowers have the strange scent of cloves. Other white-flowered members of this genus are round-leaved rein orchid, *P. orbiculata*, with a pair of round, basal leaves; coastal rein orchid, *P. greenei*, a short species only about 16" tall; and white fringed orchid, *P. blephariglottis*, with a coarsely fringed lip petal.

▲ White Prairie Clover
  5 separated petals.
  Pea-shaped flower.

▲ White Violet
  5 separated petals.

▼ White Clover
  5 separated petals. Pea-shaped flower.

▼ Bog Rein Orchid
  6 separated petal-like parts.

ASTER FAMILY

Bachelor's Buttons, *Centaurea cyanus*

Flowers: Crowded together into a head up to 1½″ wide and less than 1″ tall. Outermost disk flowers are larger than inner ones, united to form a slender tube. No ray flowers. **Stems:** Upright, branched, hairy, up to 2′ tall. **Leaves:** Alternate, simple, narrowly lanceolate, usually without teeth; hairy, up to ½″ wide. **Season:** July–Sept. **Habitat:** Open areas. **Range** (*see map*): All areas except A, B. **Family:** Aster. **Comments:** The flowers are sometimes pink, purple, or white. This is a popular species for flower gardens. Smooth star thistle, *C. americana*, has purple flowers in heads 1″–2″ high and unlobed leaves; spotted star thistle, *C. maculosa*, has pink-purple flowers in heads about ½″ high and deeply lobed leaves. Species with spines on the flower heads include caltrop, *C. calcitrapa*, with purple flowers; and yellow star thistle, *C. solstitialis*, with yellow flowers.

Blue Lettuce, *Lactuca floridana*

Flowers: Several, crowded together into numerous heads about ½″ tall. Ray flowers are blue, shallowly notched at the tip. No disk flowers. **Stems:** Upright, stout, smooth, up to 6′ tall, with milky sap. **Leaves:** Alternate, simple (but some of them deeply lobed), smooth or hairy on the veins, up to nearly 1′ long, with milky sap. **Season:** June–Oct. **Habitat:** Rich woods, roadsides. **Range** (*see map*): Areas 1–6, D, E. **Family:** Aster. **Comments:** Another wild blue lettuce is *L. biennis*, which has brownish hairs attached to the seeds rather than whitish hairs.

Chicory, *Cichorium intybus*

Flowers: Many, crowded together into heads up to 1½″ across. Ray flowers are shallowly 5-notched at the tip. No disk flowers. **Stems:** Upright, branched, hairy, up to 3′ tall, with milky sap. **Leaves:** Alternate, simple, lobed or toothed; hairy, with milky sap. **Season:** June–Oct. **Habitat:** Open soil. **Range** (*see map*): All areas except A, B. **Family:** Aster. **Comments:** This species can be used as a substitute for coffee.

RADIAL SYMMETRY

Pink Windmills, *Sisymbrium linearifolium*

Flowers: Several, in clusters (racemes), each flower up to nearly 1″ long. **Petals:** 4, separated, abruptly narrowed at the base. **Stems:** Upright, branched, smooth, up to 4½′ tall. **Leaves:** Alternate, simple, linear to lanceolate, most without teeth; smooth. **Season:** April–Oct. **Habitat:** Open areas, fields, woods. **Range** (*see map*): Areas 6–8. **Family:** Mustard. **Comments:** This species is readily recognized by its nearly 1″ petals and its narrow, usually toothless, alternate leaves.

▲ Bachelor's Buttons
Tubular flowers only.

▲ Blue Lettuce
Ray flowers only. Milky sap.

▲ Chicory
Ray flowers only. Milky sap.

Pink Windmills ▶
4 separated petals.
6 stamens.

RADIAL SYMMETRY

Common Spiderwort, *Tradescantia virginiana*

Flowers: 1 to several, in terminal clusters, up to 1½″ across. **Petals:** 3, separated, up to ¾″ long. **Stems:** Upright, up to 2½′ tall, smooth or somewhat hairy. **Leaves:** Long and slender, up to 1′ long and 1″ wide. **Season:** April–June. **Habitat:** Woods, prairies. **Range** (*see map*): Areas 1–3, 5. **Family:** Spiderwort. **Comments:** Flower color varies from blue to pink to purple to white. Broad-leaved spiderwort, *T. subaspera*, has leaves more than 1″ wide.

Wild Blue Flax, *Linum lewisii*

Flowers: Few, at the upper ends of the stems, up to 1½″ wide. **Petals:** ¾″–1″ long. **Stems:** Upright, up to 2½′ tall, smooth. **Leaves:** Very narrow, up to 1½″ long, about ⅛″ wide, with 1 vein. **Season:** May–Aug. **Habitat:** Prairies, plains. **Range** (*see map*): All areas except 2, 5, F. **Family:** Flax. **Comments:** A similar species is the cultivated flax, *L. usitatissimum*, which has petals ½″ long and broader leaves with 3 veins.

Blue Columbine, *Aquilegia caerulea*

Flowers: Few, on slender stalks, each flower up to 3½″ long and 3½″ wide. **Petals:** White, about 1″ long, prolonged backward into long, blue spurs. The petal-like sepals are blue, up to 2″ long. **Stems:** Upright, smooth or hairy, up to 2½′ tall. **Leaves:** Mostly all basal, compound, blue-green, with several round-toothed leaflets. **Season:** June–Aug. **Habitat:** Moist woods. **Range** (*see map*): Areas 7–9. **Family:** Buttercup. **Comments:** This is the state flower of Colorado. The mountain columbine, *A. saximontana*, has fewer, smaller flowers less than 1″ long.

Purple Passion-flower, *Passiflora incarnata*

Flowers: Solitary, up to 2″ across, composed of many intricate structures in addition to the petals and petal-like sepals. **Petals:** Often obscured by fringed accessory structures. **Stems:** Creeping or climbing, smooth or slightly hairy, up to 20′ long. **Leaves:** Alternate, simple, with 3 broad, toothed lobes; usually hairy, up to 5″ wide. **Season:** May–July. **Habitat:** Open areas. **Range** (*see map*): Areas 1–3, 5, 6. **Family:** Passion-flower. **Comments:** The fruit, known as a may-pop, has edible gelatinous material surrounding each seed. Yellow passion-flower, *P. lutea*, has yellow flowers less than 1″ wide.

▲ Common Spiderwort
3 separated petals.

▼ Wild Blue Flax
5 separated petals.

◄ Blue Columbine
5 separated petals.

Purple Passion-flower ▶
5 separated petals.

RADIAL SYMMETRY

Blue Iris, *Iris virginica*

Flowers: Few, terminal, up to 4″ across, the flowering tube about 1″ long. **Stems:** Upright, to 4′ tall, smooth. **Leaves:** Up to 3′ long and 1½″ wide. **Season:** April–July. **Habitat:** Wet ground. **Range** (*see map*): Areas 1–3, 5, 6, E. **Family:** Iris. **Comments:** Other large-flowered blue irises native to North America include blue flag, *I. versicolor*, with leaves purplish at base; Missouri iris, *I. missouriensis*, with blue-green leaves up to ½″ wide; and short-stemmed iris, *I. brevicaulis*, with flowers borne nearly at ground level.

Dwarf Crested Iris, *Iris cristata*

Flowers: 1 or 2 on leafless stalks up to 3″ long; each flower up to 3½″ wide, spotted with white and orange, not fragrant. **Stems:** Underground. **Leaves:** Up to 10″ long at flowering time, up to 1½″ wide. **Season:** April–June. **Habitat:** Rich woods, low woods. **Range** (*see map*): Areas 1–3, 6. **Family:** Iris. **Comments:** Another low-growing blue iris is the dwarf iris, *I. verna*, with narrower leaves and fragrant flowers.

Wild Hyacinth, *Camassia scilloides*

Flowers: Several, in an elongated leafless cluster (raceme), each flower up to 1″ across. **Petal-like Parts:** ½″–⅔″ long, equal in size, tapering to the base, 3-veined. **Flowering Stem:** Upright, up to 2′ tall. **Leaves:** All basal, up to 15″ long and ½″ wide. **Season:** April–July. **Habitat:** Prairies, woods. **Range** (*see map*): Areas 1–3, 5, 6, E. **Family:** Lily. **Comments:** The bulbs of this and most other camassias are edible. Variation in flower color ranges from blue to pale lavender and even nearly white. Camass, *C. quamash*, has petal-like parts of two different sizes; star camass, *C. leichtlinii*, has nearly equal petal-like parts with 5 veins.

Elegant Brodiaea, *Brodiaea elegans*

Flowers: Few to several, in stalked terminal clusters on a leafless stem, each flower up to 1½″ long. **Stems:** Upright, smooth, up to 2′ tall. **Leaves:** All basal, long and narrow, up to 18″ long. **Season:** April–July. **Habitat:** Fields, open areas. **Range** (*see map*): Areas 9 and 10. **Family:** Lily. **Comments:** The leaves of this plant usually wither by flowering time. Three of the six stamens are reduced to flat, white scales. Similar species include crowned brodiaea, *B. coronaria*, whose 3 reduced stamens are concave rather than flat; and grass nut, *Triteleia laxa*, a more robust plant up to 2½′ tall and with 6 normal stamens.

▲ Blue Iris
6 petal-like parts.

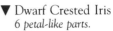
▼ Dwarf Crested Iris
6 petal-like parts.

▲ Wild Hyacinth
6 petal-like parts.

▲ Elegant Brodiaea
6 petal-like parts.

RADIAL SYMMETRY

American Bellflower, *Campanula americana*

Flowers: Several, borne along the upper part of the stem, each flower flat and about 1″ across. **Stems:** Upright, smooth or hairy, up to 7′ tall, with milky sap. **Leaves:** Alternate, simple, lanceolate to ovate-oblong, toothed; smooth or hairy, up to 6″ long. **Season:** July–Sept. **Habitat:** Moist woods. **Range** (*see map*): Areas 1–6, E. **Family:** Harebell. **Comments:** This species differs from all other bellflowers by having the petals flat, rather than forming a "bell."

Harebell, *Campanula rotundifolia*

Flowers: 1 to several, at the upper end of the stem, often nodding, bell-shaped, up to ¾″ long and ¾″ wide. **Stems:** Upright, slender, smooth or rarely hairy, seldom more than 1′ tall. **Leaves:** Basal leaves nearly round; stem leaves very narrow, up to 4″ long. **Season:** June–Sept. **Habitat:** Woods, meadows, cliffs. **Range** (*see map*): All areas except 2. **Family:** Harebell. **Comments:** The round basal leaves wither before the flowers are formed. Marsh bellflower, *C. aparinoides*, has similar, very narrow leaves on the stem, but its stems sprawl rather than grow upright; European harebell, *C. rapunculoides*, has broad, coarsely toothed leaves and flowers 1″ long; dwarf harebell, *C. uniflora*, grows only about 5″ tall and has flowers less than ½″ long.

Eastern Wild Petunia, *Ruellia caroliniensis*

Flowers: 2–3 in the axils of the leaves, 1″–2″ long. **Petals:** Lobes about ½″ long. **Stems:** Upright, smooth or hairy, up to 2′ tall. **Leaves:** Opposite, simple, lanceolate to ovate, without teeth; smooth or hairy, up to 4½″ long and 2″ wide. **Season:** May–Sept. **Habitat:** Dry woods, fields. **Range** (*see map*): Areas 1, 2, 6. **Family:** Acanthus. **Comments:** This wild petunia is recognized by having 2 or more flowers together in the leaf axils, and the lobes of the petals about ½″ long. Tall wild petunia, *R. strepens*, is similar, but the lobes of the petals are nearly 1″ long; hairy wild petunia, *R. humilis*, has 2 or more flowers per leaf axil and densely hairy leaves and stems; peduncled wild petunia, *R. pedunculata*, usually has only 1 flower per leaf axil.

Long-flowered Trumpet-flower, *Ipomopsis longiflora*

Flowers: Several, up to 2½″ long. **Petals:** 5, united into a very slender, long tube. **Stems:** Upright, much branched, up to 18″ tall. **Leaves:** Alternate, divided into 7 very narrow lobes; smooth, up to 2″ long. **Season:** March–Oct. **Habitat:** Dry soil. **Range** (*see map*): Areas 4–8. **Family:** Phlox. **Comments:** The flowers vary from pale blue to nearly white. Similar, but with smaller flowers and shorter leaves, is the lax-flowered trumpet flower, *I. laxiflora*.

▲ American Bellflower
5 united petals.

▲ Harebell
5 united petals.

▲ Eastern Wild Petunia
5 united petals.

▲ Long-flowered
Trumpet-flower
5 united petals.

RADIAL SYMMETRY

Blue Gilia, *Gilia rigidula*

Flowers: Borne singly toward the ends of the stems, bowl-shaped, about ¾" across, with a yellow center. **Stems:** Tufted, up to 15" long. **Leaves:** Alternate, pinnately divided; prickly, up to 1½" long. **Season:** April–Sept. **Habitat:** Prairies, rocky slopes. **Range** (*see map*): Areas 5–7. **Family:** Phlox. **Comments:** This gilia is readily recognized by its blue bowl-shaped flowers with a yellow center. Most gilias have long, tubular flowers. Another species with a very short floral tube is the cut-leaved gilia, *G. incisa*, which has lavender or white flowers and stems with hairy glands.

Virginia Bluebells, *Mertensia virginica*

Flowers: Several, in terminal clusters, trumpet-shaped, up to 1¼" long. **Stems:** Upright, sometimes branched, smooth, up to 2' tall. **Leaves:** Alternate, simple, oblong to oval, without teeth; smooth, up to 6" long. **Season:** March–June. **Habitat:** Rich woods. **Range** (*see map*): Areas 1–3, 5, E. **Family:** Forget-me-not. **Comments:** Other members of this genus with blue flowers less than 1" long are usually called lungworts. Tall lungwort, *M. paniculata*, has stalked leaves on the stem. Species with stalkless leaves on the stem include fringed lungwort, *M. ciliata*, with short white hairs along the leaf edges; and lance-leaved lungwort, *M. lanceolata*, with smooth leaf edges.

Soapwort Gentian, *Gentiana saponaria*

Flowers: Few to several, in dense terminal clusters, 1½"–2" long, slightly open at the tip. **Stems:** Upright, smooth or slightly hairy, up to 2½' tall. **Leaves:** Opposite, simple, lanceolate, without teeth; up to 4" long. **Season:** Sept–Oct. **Habitat:** Moist woods. **Range** (*see map*): Areas 1–3, 6. **Family:** Gentian. **Comments:** This gentian is recognized by its large, slightly open flowers. Similar gentians, whose flowers are nearly closed at the top and are referred to as closed gentians, include Andrews' closed gentian, *G. andrewsii*, with slightly pointed petals; and eastern closed gentian, *G. clausa*, with round-tipped petals.

Ivy-leaved Morning Glory, *Ipomoea hederacea*

Flowers: 1–3 in a cluster, opposite each leaf, each flower up to 1½" long. **Stems:** Twining or climbing, hairy, up to 6' long. **Leaves:** Alternate, simple, 3-lobed or unlobed, heart-shaped at the base, without teeth; hairy, up to 5" long. **Season:** June–Oct. **Habitat:** Open areas. **Range** (*see map*): Areas 1–3, 5–7, E. **Family:** Morning glory. **Comments:** This climbing morning glory is recognized by its large flowers and its 3-lobed leaves. The flowers are sometimes pink. Imperial morning glory, *I. nil*, sometimes has 3-lobed leaves, but the sepals bear long hairs; purple morning glory, *I. purpurea*, has large purple flowers 2"–3" long and unlobed leaves.

▲ Blue Gilia
  5 united petals.

▲ Virginia Bluebells
  5 united petals.

▲ Soapwort Gentian
  5 united petals.

▲ Ivy-leaved Morning Glory
  5 united petals.

BILATERAL SYMMETRY

Common Day-flower, *Commelina communis*

Flowers: Few, borne in a boat-shaped structure (spathe), each flower up to ¾" wide. **Petals:** 2 petals large and blue, 1 petal pale and much smaller. **Stems:** Sprawling or ascending, up to 18" long, smooth. **Leaves:** Alternate, simple, lanceolate; up to 5" long. **Season:** June–Oct. **Habitat:** Wet soil. **Range** (*see map*): Areas 1–6, E. **Family:** Spiderwort. **Comments:** This day-flower is recognized by its unequal petals and nearly smooth leaves. Other day-flowers with one petal much smaller than the others are creeping day-flower, *C. diffusa*, with hairy fringed leaves and all petals blue; and upright day-flower, *C. erecta*, with hairy-fringed leaves and one petal white. Virginia day-flower, *C. virginica*, has 3 blue petals, all nearly the same size.

Wild Larkspur, *Delphinium tricorne*

Flowers: Few to several, in an elongated, terminal cluster, each flower up to 1½" long. **Petals and Sepals:** All blue, with one of the sepals prolonged backward into a spur. **Stems:** Upright, smooth, unbranched, somewhat succulent, up to 15" tall. **Leaves:** Basal and alternate, deeply palmately 5- or 7-lobed; smooth; the basal leaves on longer stalks. **Season:** April–May. **Habitat:** Rich woods. **Range** (*see map*): Areas 1–3, 5, 6. **Family:** Buttercup. **Comments:** Rocky Mountain larkspur, *D. bicolor*, has flowers only about ¾" long; tall larkspur, *D. glaucum*, grows to 6' tall and has its lower 2 petals deeply lobed; Nelson's larkspur, *D. nuttallianum*, also has deeply lobed petals but is only 2½' tall.

Blue Monkshood, *Aconitum columbianum*

Flowers: Several, in terminal clusters (racemes), each flower about 1" long. **Petals and Sepals:** All petal-like, with one of the petals arched to form a hood. **Stems:** Upright, to 4½' tall, smooth or hairy. **Leaves:** Alternate, palmately lobed, up to 6" across. **Season:** June–Aug. **Habitat:** Open woods, moist meadows. **Range** (*see map*): Areas 4, 5, 7–10, C. **Family:** Buttercup. **Comments:** All parts of the plant are poisonous. Monkshood takes its name from one of the petals, which is cowl-shaped. Eastern monkshood, *A. uncinatum*, is similar but is more slender and at most only 3' tall.

Carolina Larkspur, *Delphinium carolinianum*

Flowers: Several in a terminal cluster (raceme), each flower up to 1" long. **Petals and Sepals:** All blue, with one of the sepals prolonged backward into a spur. **Stems:** Upright, to 2½' tall, hairy. **Leaves:** Basal and alternate, deeply palmately divided into narrow segments. **Season:** March–May. **Habitat:** Woods. **Range** (*see map*): Areas 1–3, 6. **Family:** Buttercup. **Comments:** Similar, but with smooth stems, is the exalted larkspur, *D. exaltatum*; wild larkspur, *D. tricorne*, has succulent stems up to 15" tall.

▲ Common Day-flower
3 separated petals.

▼ Blue Monkshood
Irregular petals.

▲ Wild Larkspur
4 separated petals

▼ Carolina Larkspur
4 separated petals.

BILATERAL SYMMETRY

Bird's-foot Violet, *Viola pedata*

Flowers: Solitary, on long leafless stalks, each flower up to 1¾" across, with one of the petals prolonged backward into a spur. **Petals:** 5, all smooth. **Stems:** Underground. **Leaves:** All basal, deeply divided into 5–11 linear or lanceolate segments; smooth. **Season:** March–June. **Habitat:** Open woods, fields, glades. **Range** (*see map*): Areas 1–3, 5, 6, E. **Family:** Violet. **Comments:** The deeply cleft leaves account for the common name of this species. In some plants, 2 of the petals are dark purple. Prairie violet, *V. pedatifida*, also has deeply divided leaves, but 3 of the petals are densely hairy on the inner surface; cleft violet, *V. triloba*, has deeply cleft leaves, but the lobes are much broader than in the other two species.

Spreading Blue Violet, *Viola adunca*

Flowers: Solitary, on long stalks arising from the leaf axils, about 1" across, with one of the petals prolonged into a spur up to ¼" long. **Stems:** Upright or spreading, up to 6" long. **Leaves:** Alternate, simple, with low rounded teeth; up to 1½" long **Season:** May–July. **Habitat:** Woods, pastures. **Range** (*see map*): All areas except 2, 5, 6. **Family:** Violet. **Comments:** This species is distinguished by its leafy stems and dark blue flowers. Dog violet, *V. conspersa*, is similar but has pale violet flowers; Walter's violet, *V. walteri*, differs by its stems, which tend to creep on the ground.

Woolly Blue Violet, *Viola sororia*

Flowers: Solitary, on long leafless stalks, up to 1¼" across, with one of the petals prolonged backward into a spur. **Stems:** Underground. **Leaves:** All basal, heart-shaped at the base, shallowly toothed; hairy, up to 4" across. **Season:** March–June. **Habitat:** Rich woods, meadows. **Range** (*see map*): Areas 1–6. **Family:** Violet. **Comments:** Woolly blue violet is characterized by its having heart-shaped leaves. Common blue violet, *V. papilionacea*, is similar but lacks hairs on the leaves. Marsh blue violet, *V. cucullata*, has smooth leaves but there are club-shaped hairs on the inner surface of some of the petals.

Winter Vetch, *Vicia villosa*

Flowers: Several, in one-sided elongated clusters, each flower about ½" long. **Petals:** 5, arranged to form a typical pea-shaped flower. **Stems:** Spreading to ascending, up to 2' long, with spreading hairs. **Leaves:** Alternate, divided into 10–24 leaflets; the leaflets narrowly oblong, without teeth, up to ¾" long. **Season:** June–Aug. **Habitat:** Roadsides, fields. **Range** (*see map*): All areas except B. **Family:** Pea. **Comments:** Another vetch with several flowers in elongated clusters is smooth vetch, *V. dasycarpa*, with few or no hairs on the stem.

▲ Bird's-foot Violet
5 separated petals.

▼ Woolly Blue Violet
5 separated petals.

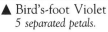

▲ Spreading Blue Violet
5 separated petals.

Winter Vetch ▶
5 separated petals.
Pea-shaped flower.

BLUE–VIOLET

BILATERAL SYMMETRY

Silverstem Lupine, *Lupinus argenteus*

Flowers: Several, in terminal clusters (racemes), each flower ⅓″–½″ long. **Stems:** Upright, up to 2′ tall, covered with silvery hairs. **Leaves:** Alternate, palmately compound, with 7–9 silvery-hairy leaflets. **Season:** June–Oct. **Habitat:** Plains, open woods. **Range** (*see map*): Areas 4, 5, 7–10, C, D. **Family:** Pea. **Comments:** There are about 150 species of lupines in North America. This species is distinguished by its silvery-silky leaves and stems. Because of their beauty, lupines are prized as garden plants.

Texas Bluebonnet, *Lupinus texensis*

Flowers: Several, in terminal clusters (racemes), each flower ⅓″–½″ long. **Stems:** Upright, up to 16″ tall, hairy. **Leaves:** Alternate, palmately compound; the leaflets 5 or 7, oblanceolate, toothless, pointed at the tip, up to 1″ long. **Season:** March–May. **Habitat:** Roadsides. **Range** (*see map*): Area 6. **Family:** Pea. **Comments:** Although native to Texas, the Texas bluebonnet has become much more abundant through the activities of the state highway department and Texas garden clubs. Shy lupine, *T. subcarnosus*, the state flower of Texas, has round-tipped leaflets.

Horsemint, *Monarda bradburiana*

Flowers: Several, crowded into a solitary head up to 3″ across, each flower up to 1″ long. **Petals:** 5, united below, 2-lipped. **Stems:** Upright, usually unbranched, sometimes hairy, square, up to 18″ tall. **Leaves:** Opposite, simple, ovate, coarsely toothed; hairy, without stalks. **Season:** April–May. **Habitat:** Woods. **Range** (*see map*): Areas 1–3, 5, 6. **Family:** Mint. **Comments:** A similar *Monarda* with bright red flowers is oswego tea, *M. didyma*.

Pickerelweed, *Pontederia cordata*

Flowers: Several, crowded into an elongated spike up to 6″ long, each flower 1″ across. **Petal-like Parts:** 6, unequal in size, united at the base. **Stems:** Upright, up to 3′ tall, smooth. **Leaves:** Basal and alternate, simple, ovate to lanceolate, heart-shaped at the base, without teeth; smooth, up to 8″ long. **Season:** June–Nov. **Habitat:** Around lakes and ponds, in mud. **Range** (*see map*): Areas 1–3, 6, E, F. **Family:** Pickerelweed. **Comments:** This is one of the most handsome wetland wildflowers, distinguished by its dense spike of blue flowers. The leaves vary from ovate to lanceolate.

▲ Silverstem Lupine
  5 separated petals. Pea-shaped flower.

Texas Bluebonnet ▶
  5 separated petals. Pea-shaped flower.

▲ Horsemint
  5 united petals.

Pickerelweed ▶
  6 united petal-like parts.

BILATERAL SYMMETRY

Blue-eyed Mary, *Collinsia verna*

Flowers: Several, in the axils of the upper leaves, up to ⅔″ long, on slender stalks up to 1″ long. **Petals:** 2 white upper petals, 3 blue lower petals; all petals united below. **Stems:** Upright, usually smooth, up to 1′ tall. **Leaves:** Opposite, simple, sometimes finely hairy; the lower leaves are ovate, toothed or toothless; the middle and upper leaves are narrower and toothed. **Season:** April–May. **Habitat:** Low woods. **Range** (*see map*): Areas 1–3, 5, 6, E. **Family:** Snapdragon. **Comments:** Where this species is common, it can cover several acres in an amazing display of color. Violet collinsia, *C. violacea*, has similar-sized flowers that are violet and white; small-flowered collinsia, *C. parviflora*, has blue and white flowers only ¼″ long.

Wild Sage, *Salvia lyrata*

Flowers: Usually 6 per cluster, with several clusters forming a terminal spike, each flower up to 1″ long. **Petals:** 5, united below, the lobes arranged in 2 lips. **Stems:** Upright, usually unbranched, hairy, up to 2′ tall. **Leaves:** Basal and opposite, hairy; the basal leaves are pinnately lobed, up to 8″ long on long stalks; the stem leaves are smaller, pinnately lobed to merely toothed, without stalks. **Season:** April–June. **Habitat:** Rich woods. **Range** (*see map*): Areas 1–3, 5, 6. **Family:** Mint. **Comments:** The pinnately lobed basal leaves distinguish this species from other sages. European sage, *S. nemorosa*, usually lacks basal leaves; reflexed sage, *S. reflexa*, has lanceolate stem leaves and only 2 flowers in a cluster; blue sage, *S. pitcheri*, has linear to lanceolate stem leaves and 6–12 flowers in a cluster.

Sand Beardtongue, *Penstemon buckleyi*

Flowers: Several, crowded into a terminal spike, each flower up to ⅔″ long. **Petals:** 5, 2-lipped, united below. **Stems:** Upright, unbranched, smooth, up to 18″ tall. **Leaves:** Opposite, simple, thick, without teeth; smooth, somewhat whitish, up to 3″ long. **Season:** March–April. **Habitat:** Sandy areas. **Range** (*see map*): Areas 5 and 6. **Family:** Snapdragon. **Comments:** This species is able to tolerate blowing sand. Fendler's beardtongue, *P. fendleri*, has branched stems and slightly larger, pinkish flowers.

Blue Cardinal Flower, *Lobelia siphilitica*

Flowers: Crowded into elongated terminal clusters (racemes), each flower about 1″ long. **Petals:** 5, split into 2 lips. **Stems:** Upright, smooth or hairy, up to 4½′ tall. **Leaves:** Alternate, simple, oblong to lanceolate, toothed; smooth or hairy, up to 5″ long. **Season:** Aug–Oct. **Habitat:** Wet ground. **Range** (*see map*): Areas 1–6, 8, E. **Family:** Lobelia. **Comments:** This is one of the most beautiful wildflowers of wetlands. Hairy blue cardinal flower, *L. puberula*, has similar flowers but is smaller and hairier; spiked lobelia, *L. spicata*, is very slender, with pale blue flowers about ½″ long.

▲ Blue-eyed Mary
  5 united petals.

▼ Sand Beardtongue
  5 united petals.

▲ Wild Sage
  5 united petals.

▼ Blue Cardinal Flower
  5 united petals.

ASTER FAMILY

Pale Coneflower, *Echinacea pallida*

Flowers: Crowded into solitary heads up to 4″ across. Ray flowers are pale to deep purple, up to 3″ long, slender. Disk flowers are dark purple, tubular. **Stems:** Upright, hairy, up to 3′ tall. **Leaves:** Basal and alternate, linear to elliptic, simple, usually without teeth; hairy, up to 8″ long. **Season:** May–Aug. **Habitat:** Prairies, glades. **Range** (*see map*): Areas 2, 3, 5, 6, E. **Family:** Aster. **Comments:** The color of the rays of this species varies from pale pink to deep purple. Purple coneflower, *E. purpurea*, is similar but has broader, toothed leaves and usually more reddish purple flowers; narrow-leaved coneflower, *E. angustifolia*, grows only about 1½′ tall and has ray flowers about 1½″ long.

Daisy Fleabane, *Erigeron philadelphicus*

Flowers: Many, crowded into several heads up to 1″ across. Ray flowers are pink or white, very narrow, more than 100 per head. Disk flowers are yellow, tubular. **Stems:** Upright, branched, smooth or hairy, up to 3′ tall. **Leaves:** Alternate, simple, obovate, toothed; smooth or hairy, up to 3″ long. **Season:** May–June. **Habitat:** Fields, open areas. **Range** (*see map*): All areas except A. **Family:** Aster. **Comments:** This species is recognized by its numerous narrow, pink or white rays. Robin's plantain, *E. pulchellus*, has hollow flowering stems and fewer than 100 wider rays per head; slender fleabane, *E. tenuis*, has numerous narrow, blue rays; tufted fleabane, *E. compositus*, grows only 6″ tall and has pinnately lobed basal leaves.

New England Aster, *Aster novae-angliae*

Flowers: Crowded into numerous terminal heads up to 2½″ across. Ray flowers are usually rose-pink, up to 100 per head, ½″–1″ long. Disk flowers are yellow, tubular. **Stems:** Upright, hairy, up to 8′ tall. **Leaves:** Alternate, simple, lanceolate, partially encircling the stem at their base, without teeth; with rough hairs, up to 5″ long. **Season:** July–Oct. **Habitat:** Open areas, prairies, woods. **Range** (*see map*): Areas 1–9, D, E. **Family:** Aster. **Comments:** Other asters with stem leaves partially encircling the stem include spreading aster, *A. patens*, with 15–25 rays per head; and northern aster, *A. modestus*, with glandular hairs on the upper stem.

Rush Pink, *Lygodesmia grandiflora*

Flowers: Crowded into solitary heads up to 2″ across. Ray flowers are usually 5–10 per head, up to 1″ long, 5-toothed at tip. No disk flowers. **Stems:** Upright, smooth, up to 20″ tall, with milky sap. **Leaves:** Alternate, simple, linear, without teeth; smooth, up to 4″ long, with milky sap. **Season:** May–June. **Habitat:** Dry soil, plains. **Range** (*see map*): Areas 4, 7–9. **Family:** Aster. **Comments:** The flowers are much larger than one would expect for the size of the plant. The narrow leaves give the plant the appearance of a rush when not in flower. Texas skeleton plant, *L. ramosissima*, has lobed leaves; early skeleton plant, *L. juncea*, has smaller flowering heads up to 1″ across, usually with only 5 rays.

▲ Pale Coneflower
Ray and disk flowers.

Daisy Fleabane ▶
Ray and disk flowers.

▲ New England Aster
Ray and disk flowers.

▲ Rush Pink
Ray flowers only. Milky sap.

ASTER FAMILY

Pink Pussytoes, *Antennaria rosea*

Flowers: Many, in terminal pink or rose heads, up to ⅛" across, the pollen-bearing flowers borne on separate plants from the pistil-bearing plants. No ray flowers. Disk flowers are tubular, surrounded by pink or rose leaf-like structures (bracts). **Stems:** Mat-forming, up to 15" long, hairy. **Leaves:** Basal and alternate, hairy; the basal leaves are oblanceolate, up to 1" long; the stem leaves are oblong to linear. **Season:** May–Aug. **Habitat:** Prairies, dry or moist valleys, mountains. **Range** (*see map*): Areas 3–5, 7–10, A–E. **Family:** Aster. **Comments:** *A. plantaginifolia*, an eastern species, has white flower heads and basal leaves more than 1" long.

Baldwin's Ironweed, *Vernonia baldwinii*

Flowers: Many, crowded into several heads ½" across, each head encircled from below by purplish, pointed, leaf-like structures (bracts). No ray flowers. Disk flowers are tubular, 5-lobed. **Stems:** Upright, branched or unbranched, hairy, up to 6' tall. **Leaves:** Alternate, simple, ovate to lanceolate, toothed; hairy, up to 6" long. **Season:** July–Sept. **Habitat:** Prairies, fields, woods. **Range** (*see map*): Areas 2, 3, 5, 6. **Family:** Aster. **Comments:** Missouri ironweed, *V. missurica*, is very similar, except for its round-tipped bracts and softly hairy leaves; tall ironweed, *V. gigantea*, has round-tipped bracts and nearly smooth leaves.

Nodding Thistle, *Carduus nutans*

Flowers: Many, crowded into solitary heads up to 2½" across, the heads nodding and encircled from below by sharp-pointed leaf-like structures (bracts). No ray flowers. Disk flowers are tubular, fragrant. **Stems:** Upright, branched, hairy, usually bordered by a spiny wing, up to 5' tall. **Leaves:** Alternate, simple, deeply lobed; prickly throughout, up to 6" long. **Season:** June–Oct. **Habitat:** Roadsides, fields. **Range** (*see map*): Areas 1–10, C–F. **Family:** Aster. **Comments:** This species usually becomes an aggressive weed. Spiny musk thistle, *C. acanthoides*, has wickedly spiny leaves and stems, flowering heads about 1" across, and leaves smooth or with a few long hairs; wavy musk thistle, *C. crispus*, has usually spiny leaves and stems, flowering heads about 1" across, and leaves covered by short hairs.

Field Thistle, *Cirsium discolor*

Flowers: Many, crowded into heads up to 2" across, encircled from below by leaf-like structures (bracts), some of which are tipped with bristles. No ray flowers. Disk flowers are tubular. **Stems:** Upright, branched, hairy, up to 8' tall. **Leaves:** Alternate, simple, deeply divided into many jagged, prickly tipped lobes; with white hairs on the lower surface, up to 1' long. **Season:** Aug–Oct. **Habitat:** Fields, woods, open areas. **Range** (*see map*): Areas 1–5, D, E. **Family:** Aster. **Comments:** Bull thistle, *C. vulgare*, has spiny stems, spiny bracts, and heads up to 2½" across; tall thistle, *C. altissimum*, has prickly bracts, and its leaves have white hairs and are not pinnately divided; Canada thistle, *C. arvense*, lacks prickly bracts.

▲ Pink Pussytoes
Tubular flowers only.

▲ Nodding Thistle
Tubular flowers only.

▲ Baldwin's Ironweed
Tubular flowers only.

Field Thistle ▶
Tubular flowers only.

ASTER FAMILY

Prairie Blazing Star, *Liatris pycnostachya*

Flowers: Several, crowded into short heads, with the numerous heads densely grouped into cylindrical terminal spikes up to 1½' long, with each head up to ½" long. No ray flowers. Disk flowers are tubular, 5-lobed. **Stems:** Upright, unbranched, hairy, up to 5' tall. **Leaves:** Alternate, simple, narrowly lanceolate, without teeth; hairy, up to ½" across. **Season:** July–Sept. **Habitat:** Prairies. **Range** (*see map*): Areas 1–6. **Family:** Aster. **Comments:** This species is distinguished by its long, thick, cylindrical spikes and hairy stems. Dotted blazing star, *L. punctata*, has cylindrical spikes and smooth stems; rough blazing star, *L. aspera*, has flowers in distinct rounded heads all the same size and encircled from below by round-tipped leaf-like structures (bracts); large-headed blazing star, *L. ligulistylis*, has flowers in distinct rounded heads (the terminal head is the largest) and round-tipped bracts; squarrose blazing star, *L. squarrosa*, has flowers in distinct rounded heads and has pointed bracts.

Joe-pye-weed, *Eupatorium fistulosum*

Flowers: Several, in small heads arranged in large round-topped clusters, each individual head up to ¼" long. No ray flowers. Disk flowers are tubular, 5-lobed. **Stems:** Robust, purple, smooth, hollow, up to 10' tall. **Leaves:** Whorled in groups of 4–7, simple, elliptic-lanceolate; hairy, up to 8" long. **Season:** July–Sept. **Habitat:** Wet ground. **Range** (*see map*): Areas 1–3, 6. **Family:** Aster. **Comments:** This species is distinguished by its hollow purple stems and round-topped flower clusters.

Mist Flower, *Eupatorium coelestinum*

Flowers: Several, crowded into small heads, the heads grouped into terminal clusters. No ray flowers. Disk flowers are tubular, 5-lobed. **Stems:** Upright, to 2' tall, with short hairs. **Leaves:** Opposite, simple, ovate, round-toothed; up to 4" long. **Season:** July–Oct. **Habitat:** Wet ground. **Range** (*see map*): Areas 1–3, 5, 6. **Family:** Aster. **Comments:** This species, shorter than most members of the genus, has a strong resemblance to the garden plant ageratum. Swamp mist flower, *E. incarnatum*, has light pink flowers and triangular-shaped leaves.

RADIAL SYMMETRY

Tall Spiderwort, *Tradescantia ohiensis*

Flowers: Few, in a terminal cluster, each flower up to 1½" across. **Petals:** 3, separated, nearly 1" long. **Sepals:** 3, hairy at the tip. **Stems:** Upright, smooth, bluish, up to 5' tall. **Leaves:** Alternate, simple, narrowly lanceolate, without teeth. **Season:** April–June. **Habitat:** Prairies, open woods, fields. **Range** (*see map*): Areas 1–3, 5, 6, E. **Family:** Spiderwort. **Comments:** This spiderwort is known by its completely smooth stems and leaves. Prairie spiderwort, *T. bracteata*, lacks the bluish tinge to its stems; western spiderwort, *T. occidentalis*, has sepals hairy all over.

▲ Joe-pye-weed
Tubular flowers only.

▲ Prairie Blazing Star
Tubular flowers only.

▲ Mist Flower
Tubular flowers only.

▲ Tall Spiderwort
3 separated petals.

GROUPED FLOWERS APPEAR SINGLE

Umbrella-wort, *Allionia incarnata*

Flowers: In clusters of 3, with the entire cluster resembling a single flower. **Petal-like Parts:** United, 4- or 5-lobed, ¼" long or longer. **Stems:** Sprawling on ground, with sticky hairs, up to 3' long. **Leaves:** Opposite, simple, oval to oblong, without teeth; hairy, up to 2" long. **Season:** April–Sept. **Habitat:** Dry, often rocky soils. **Range** (*see map*): Areas 6–8, 10. **Family:** Four-o'clock. **Comments:** The sticky-hairy stems and larger flowers differentiate this species. Smooth umbrella-wort, *A. choisyi*, usually lacks sticky-hairy stems and has petal-like parts less than ¼" long.

Colorado Four-o'clock, *Mirabilis multiflora*

Flowers: Solitary or few, in a cluster. **Petal-like Parts:** Trumpet-shaped, up to 2½" long. **Stems:** Spreading or upright, up to 1½' long, hairy. **Leaves:** Opposite, simple, ovate to oblong, rather thick and succulent, without teeth; smooth or hairy, up to 3½" long. **Season:** April–Sept. **Habitat:** Dry, often rocky soils. **Range** (*see map*): Areas 5–8, 10. **Family:** Four-o'clock. **Comments:** Spreading four-o'clock, *M. oxybaphoides*, has petal-like parts about ½" long.

RADIAL SYMMETRY

Teasel, *Dipsacus fullonum*

Flowers: Crowded into dense terminal heads up to 4" long, each flower ½"–⅔" long, encircled from below by sharp-pointed, prickly, leaf-like structures (bracts). **Petals:** 4, united below. **Stems:** Upright, prickly, up to 6' tall. **Leaves:** Opposite, simple, lanceolate, without teeth; prickly on the main vein, up to 12" long. **Season:** July–Sept. **Habitat:** Roadsides, open areas. **Range** (*see map*): Areas 1–6, 8–10. **Family:** Teasel. **Comments:** The bristly heads were used in the past to comb wool. Cleft teasel, *D. laciniatus*, has pinnately divided leaves.

Wild Verbena, *Verbena canadensis*

Flowers: Several, usually in terminal spikes, each flower up to ¾" across. **Petals:** 5, notched at tip, united below. **Stems:** Sprawling to upright, branched, hairy, up to 1½' long. **Leaves:** Opposite, simple, pinnately lobed; hairy, up to 3" long. **Season:** March–Aug. **Habitat:** Prairies, woods. **Range** (*see map*): Areas 1–3, 5, 6. **Family:** Vervain. **Comments:** This is a large genus, with many of the species having tiny flowers. Other showy-flowered species include Dakota vervain, *V. bipinnatifida*, with greatly divided leaves and flowers about ½" across.

▲ Umbrella-wort
Grouped flowers appear single.

▲ Colorado Four-o'clock
Grouped flowers appear single.

▲ Teasel
4 united petals.

▲ Wild Verbena
5 united petals.

RADIAL SYMMETRY

Hooker's Onion, *Allium acuminatum*

Flowers: 12–30 in a terminal cluster (umbel) on a leafless stem. **Petal-like Parts:** 6, pointed and curved back at the tip, about ½″ long. **Stems:** Upright, leafless, up to 12″ tall. **Leaves:** All basal, long and narrow, up to 6″ long. **Season:** May–July. **Habitat:** Dry, open areas. **Range** (*see map*): Areas 7–10, C. **Family:** Lily. **Comments:** The slender, curved-back tips of the petal-like parts distinguish this species. Drummond's wild onion, *A. drummondii*, has flowers less than ½″ long, petal-like parts that do not curve back at the tip, and leaves about as long as the flowering stem; Geyer's onion, *A. geyeri*, is similar to Drummond's onion, but its leaves are shorter than the flowering stem.

Nodding Onion, *Allium cernuum*

Flowers: Few to many, in a nodding, terminal cluster (umbel). **Petal-like Parts:** 6, separated, rounded at the tip, about ⅙″ long. **Stems:** Upright, leafless, up to 1½′ tall. **Leaves:** All basal, linear, up to ¼″ wide. **Season:** July–Oct. **Habitat:** Rocky soil, wooded slopes. **Range** (*see map*): Areas 1–9, C–E. **Family:** Lily. **Comments:** The nodding cluster of flowers differentiates this species. Prairie onion, *A. stellatum*, has erect clusters at maturity and pointed petal-like parts of uniform color; Arizona onion, *A. macropetalum*, has erect clusters and pointed petal-like parts with a darker central stripe.

Rosy Twisted-stalk, *Streptopus roseus*

Flowers: Solitary and hanging from the axil of each leaf on twisted stalks, each flower up to ½″ long. **Petal-like Parts:** 6, separated, straight. **Stems:** Upright, hairy, up to 16″ tall. **Leaves:** Alternate, simple, broadly lanceolate, without teeth; hairy, up to 4″ long. **Season:** June–July. **Habitat:** Moist woods, damp soil. **Range** (*see map*): Areas 1–3, 9, A, C–F. **Family:** Lily. **Comments:** The twisted flower stalks readily segregate this genus. Wild mandarin, *S. amplexifolius*, has petal-like parts that curve back strongly.

Purple Loosestrife, *Lythrum salicaria*

Flowers: Many, in slender terminal spikes up to 1′ long, each flower up to ½″ long. **Petals:** 6, separated, strongly tapering to the base, ½″ long. **Stems:** Upright, smooth or hairy, up to 4′ tall. **Leaves:** Opposite, simple, lanceolate to oblong, without teeth; smooth or hairy, up to 4″ long, without stalks. **Season:** July–Sept. **Habitat:** Wet ground. **Range** (*see map*): Areas 1–6, C–F. **Family:** Loosestrife. **Comments:** This handsome species is an aggressive weed and tends to destroy wetland habitats. Winged loosestrife, *L. alatum*, has smooth, square stems and petals about ¼″ long.

▲ Hooker's Onion
6 *separated petal-like parts.*

▼ Nodding Onion
6 *separated petal-like parts.*

▼ Purple Loosestrife
6 *separated petal-like parts.*

▲ Rosy Twisted-stalk
6 *separated petal-like parts.*

RADIAL SYMMETRY

Ookow, *Dichelostemma pulchellum*

Flowers: 6–16, showy, in a dense cluster (umbel). **Petal-like Parts:** 6, ½"–⅓" long, united below into a short tube, violet. **Stems:** Upright, leafless, smooth, up to 3' tall. **Leaves:** All basal, long and narrow, pointed. **Season:** Jan–May. **Habitat:** Open areas. **Range** (*see map*): Areas 7–10. **Family:** Lily. **Comments:** Forktooth ookow, *D. congesta,* has blue-violet flowers; firecracker flower, *D. ida-maia,* has red flowers.

Beehive Cactus, *Coryphantha vivipara*

Flowers: Solitary, up to 2½" across. **Petal-like Parts:** Numerous, separated. **Stems:** Ovoid to cylindrical, up to 3½" in diameter, growing in clumps, with 3–10 central spines and 12–40 radial spines per central area (areole). **Season:** May–July. **Habitat:** Dry soil, deserts. **Range** (*see map*): Areas 3–10, C, D. **Family:** Cactus. **Comments:** The flowers of this attractive cactus range from pink to white to yellow.

Beavertail Prickly Pear, *Opuntia basilaris*

Flowers: Solitary, up to 2½" across. **Petals:** Numerous, separated. **Stems:** Flat oval pads up to 14" long and 7" wide, gray-green, with central areas (areoles) surrounded by ¼" spines. **Season:** March–June. **Habitat:** Deserts, dry soil. **Range** (*see map*): Areas 7, 8, 10. **Family:** Cactus. **Comments:** The shape of the large fleshy stems ("pads") accounts for the common name of this cactus. Although the absence of long spines gives this species the appearance of being harmless, the small spines that ring the areoles can cause problems. The flowers are sometimes yellow.

Rainbow Cactus, *Echinocereus rigidissimus*

Flowers: Solitary, up to 5½" across. **Petals:** Numerous, separated. **Stems:** Cylindrical, up to 4" wide, with bands of colorful spines, the spines ½" long and in clusters. **Season:** June–Aug. **Habitat:** Dry, rocky areas. **Range** (*see map*): Area 7. **Family:** Cactus. **Comments:** The bands of colorful spines account for the common name. The flowers are sometimes yellow.

▲ Ookow
  6 united petal-like parts.

▲ Beehive Cactus
  Many separated
  petal-like parts.

▲ Beavertail Prickly Pear
  Many separated petal-like parts.

▼ Rainbow Cactus
  Many separated petal-like parts.

RADIAL SYMMETRY

Winged Meadow Beauty, *Rhexia virginica*

Flowers: Few, in terminal clusters, each flower up to 1½" across. **Petals:** 4, separated. **Stems:** Upright, 4-sided, somewhat 4-winged, hairy, up to 2' tall. **Leaves:** Opposite, simple, narrowly ovate, toothed, rounded at base; smooth or hairy, up to 2½" long, without a stalk. **Season:** May–Oct. **Habitat:** Moist, open soil. **Range** (*see map*): Areas 1–3, 6, E, F. **Family:** Meadow Beauty. **Comments:** Common meadow beauty, *R. mariana*, has leaves tapering at the base, with hairy, scarcely 4-sided stems; stalked meadow beauty, *R. petiolata*, has smooth stems.

Purple Rocket, *Hesperis matronalis*

Flowers: Several, in terminal clusters (racemes), each flower about 1" across, fragrant. **Petals:** Purple, about 1" long. **Stems:** Upright, sometimes branched, to 3' tall. **Leaves:** Alternate, simple, lanceolate, toothed; hairy, up to 2" long. **Season:** May–July. **Habitat:** Roadsides. **Range** (*see map*): All areas except 6, 7, B. **Family:** Mustard. **Comments:** This handsome, tall perennial is a popular plant for flower gardens.

Pink Cress, *Cardamine douglasii*

Flowers: Several, in terminal clusters, each flower nearly 1" across. **Petals:** 4, separated. **Stems:** Upright, smooth or hairy, up to 18" tall. **Leaves:** Basal and alternate, ovate, coarsely toothed or shallowly lobed; smooth or hairy. **Season:** March–May. **Habitat:** Moist woods. **Range** (*see map*): Areas 1–6, D, E. **Family:** Mustard. **Comments:** The very similar bulbous cress, *C. bulbosa*, has white flowers.

Deerhorn Clarkia, *Clarkia pulchella*

Flowers: Few, in a terminal cluster, each flower up to 2" across. **Petals:** 4, separated, deeply 3-lobed, with the middle lobe much wider than the lateral lobes. **Stems:** Upright, smooth, up to 2' tall. **Leaves:** Alternate, simple, linear, up to 1½" long. **Season:** May–July. **Habitat:** Woods. **Range** (*see map*): Areas 4, 9, C. **Family:** Evening Primrose. **Comments:** Several clarkias have 3-lobed petals. Others include lovely clarkia, *C. concinna*, with all 3 lobes about the same in size; and narrow-lobed clarkia, *C. xantiana*, with the middle lobe much narrower than the lateral lobes.

▲ Winged Meadow Beauty
4 separated petals. 8 stamens.

▲ Purple Rocket
4 separated petals. 6 stamens.

Deerhorn Clarkia ▶
4 separated petals. 8 stamens.

◀ Pink Cress
4 separated petals. 6 stamens.

RADIAL SYMMETRY

Fireweed, *Epilobium angustifolium*

Flowers: Several, in terminal clusters (racemes), each flower up to 1½″ across. **Petals:** 4, separated, up to ¾″ long, narrowing to the base. **Stems:** Upright, smooth, up to 8′ tall. **Leaves:** Alternate, simple, narrowly lanceolate, without teeth; usually smooth, up to 6″ long. **Season:** June–Sept. **Habitat:** Open areas. **Range** (*see map*): Areas 1, 3–5, 7–10, A. **Family:** Evening Primrose. **Comments:** The common name alludes to the rapidity with which this species invades burned areas. It often grows in dense masses. Marsh willow herb, *E. palustre,* has toothless leaves and hairy stems; Hornemann's willow herb, *E. hornemannii,* has toothed leaves and petals about ½″ long; common willow herb, *E. coloratum,* has toothed leaves and petals ¼″ long; ciliate willow herb, *E. ciliatum,* has toothed leaves and petals ⅙″ long.

Pink Evening Primrose, *Oenothera speciosa*

Flowers: Solitary, in the upper leaf axils, up to 3″ across. **Petals:** 4, separated, white before usually turning pink, broadly rounded. **Stems:** Upright or sprawling, hairy, up to 2′ tall. **Leaves:** Alternate, simple, with or without a few narrow lobes; hairy, up to 3½″ long. **Season:** May–July. **Habitat:** Open soil. **Range** (*see map*): Areas 1–3, 5–7, 10. **Family:** Evening Primrose. **Comments:** The large, usually pink flowers and the often lobed leaves distinguish this attractive species. Nuttall's evening primrose, *O. nuttallii,* has very narrow leaves without lobes.

Pussy Paws, *Calyptridium umbellatum*

Flowers: Densely crowded into terminal clusters, becoming papery at maturity. **Petals:** 4, separated, withering early, up to ¼″ long, surpassed by the nearly transparent sepals. **Stems:** Creeping, branched, hairy, up to 10″ long. **Leaves:** Basal, forming a rosette, broadened at the tip, up to 3″ long. **Season:** May–Aug. **Habitat:** Woods, usually under conifers. **Range** (*see map*): Areas 8–10, C. **Family:** Portulaca. **Comments:** The flower clusters have a resemblance to the bottom of a cat's foot.

Bitterroot, *Lewisia rediviva*

Flowers: Solitary, up to 3″ across, nearly concealing the leaves. **Petals:** 12–18, separated, tapering to the base. **Stems:** Up to 2″ tall. **Leaves:** Basal, succulent, linear, up to 2″ long. **Season:** May–July. **Habitat:** Open areas. **Range** (*see map*): Areas 4, 7–10, C. **Family:** Portulaca. **Comments:** This is a remarkable species with large flowers obscuring the tufts of succulent leaves. It is the state flower of Montana. Siskiyou lewisia, *L. cotyledon,* has a rosette of basal leaves but only 8–10 petals per flower.

◀ Fireweed
4 separated petals. 8 stamens.

▲ Pink Evening Primrose
4 separated petals. 8 stamens.

◀ Pussy Paws
4 separated petals. 3 stamens.

▼ Bitterroot
12–18 separated petals.

RADIAL SYMMETRY

Wild Crane's-bill, *Geranium carolinianum*

Flowers: Usually 2 in a group, each flower up to ½″ across. **Petals:** 5, separated, pink but with conspicuous lines. **Stems:** Spreading to upright, much branched, hairy, up to 15″ long. **Leaves:** Basal and alternate, deeply palmately divided into 5 to 9 toothed lobes; hairy, up to 3″ across. **Season:** May–Aug. **Habitat:** Dry woods, fields, roadsides. **Range** (*see map*): Areas 1–10, C–E. **Family:** Geranium. **Comments:** Similar crane's-bills are Bicknell's crane's-bill, *G. bicknellii*, with leaves very deeply 5-lobed; and small crane's-bill, *G. pusillum*, with smaller flowers.

Wild Geranium, *Geranium maculatum*

Flowers: Few, in terminal clusters, each flower up to 1½″ across. **Petals:** 5, separated, with dark veins, up to ¾″ long. **Stems:** Upright, branched, hairy, up to 1½′ tall. **Leaves:** Hairy; the basal leaves are 3- to 5-lobed, up to 5″ wide, on long stalks; the 2 leaves on the stem are opposite, short-stalked. **Season:** April–June. **Habitat:** Rich woods. **Range** (*see map*): Areas 1–6, E. **Family:** Geranium. **Comments:** The large flowers and the pair of leaves on the stem distinguish this species.

Purple Oxalis, *Oxalis violacea*

Flowers: 2–10 on long, leafless stalks, each flower nearly 1″ across. **Petals:** 5, separated, rounded at the tip. **Stems:** Upright, slender, smooth, unbranched, up to 8″ tall. **Leaves:** All basal, divided into 3 leaflets; the leaflets are notched at the tip, smooth, and often purple, at least on the lower surface. **Season:** April–July. **Habitat:** Woods, fields, dry soil. **Range** (*see map*): Areas 1–9. **Family:** Wood Sorrel. **Comments:** Other pink or purple sorrels include red sorrel, *O. rubra*, with red-spotted leaflets; notched sorrel, *O. corymbosa*, with leaflets deeply notched; violet sorrel, *O. amplifolia*, with V-shaped leaflets; and redwood sorrel, *O. oregana*, with rusty-hairy stems and leaflets.

Red Maids, *Calandrinia ciliata*

Flowers: Few, in the leaf axils, up to ½″ across. **Petals:** 5, separated. **Stems:** Spreading or upright, somewhat succulent, up to 15″ long. **Leaves:** Alternate, narrow, without teeth; somewhat succulent, up to 3″ long. **Season:** April–May. **Habitat:** Open areas. **Range** (*see map*): Areas 7, 9, 10, C. **Family:** Portulaca. **Comments:** This showy little plant is distinguished by its bright flowers and succulent leaves and stems. Desert calandrinia, *C. ambigua*, is a succulent with white petals and flowers in a cluster (umbel).

▲ Wild Crane's-bill
   5 separated petals. 10 stamens.

▼ Wild Geranium
   5 separated petals. 10 stamens.

▼ Purple Oxalis
   5 separated petals. 10 stamens.

▼ Red Maids
   5 separated petals. Usually 10 stamens.

RADIAL SYMMETRY

Stork's-bill, *Erodium cicutarium*

Flowers: Few, in terminal clusters (umbels), each flower up to ½" across. **Petals:** 5, separated. **Stems:** Upright, branched, hairy, to 1' long. **Leaves:** Basal and alternate, pinnately compound with several toothed or lobed leaflets; hairy. **Season:** April–Sept. **Habitat:** Fields, lawns. **Range** (*see map*): All areas except A, B. **Family:** Geranium. **Comments:** The elongated fruits account for the common name. The 5 stamens distinguish this species from the genus *Geranium*, which has 10 stamens. Texas stork's-bill, *E. texanum*, has simple or palmately divided leaves.

Flower-of-an-hour, *Talinum calycinum*

Flowers: Several, in a cluster at the tip of a leafless stem, each flower up to 1½" across. **Petals:** 5, separated, withering after about an hour. **Stems:** Up to 12" tall, leafless, bearing flowers at the tip. **Leaves:** All basal, succulent, cylindrical, up to 4" long. **Season:** May–July. **Habitat:** Rocky ledges, glades. **Range** (*see map*): Areas 2, 3, 5, 6. **Family:** Portulaca. **Comments:** The flowers of all 17 species in North America last only about an hour. All species have succulent, cylindrical, basal leaves. Small flower-of-an-hour, *T. parviflorum*, has flowers only about ½" across.

Scarlet Smartweed, *Polygonum amphibium*

Flowers: Many, in thick terminal spikes up to 6" long and ½" thick, each flower about ¼" long. **Petals:** None, but the 5 sepals are petal-like, separated. **Stems:** Floating or upright, smooth or hairy, up to 4' tall. **Leaves:** Alternate, simple, lanceolate to ovate, toothless; smooth or hairy, up to 8" long. **Season:** June–Oct. **Habitat:** In water and mud. **Range** (*see map*): All areas except A. **Family:** Smartweed. **Comments:** This smartweed is distinguished by its very thick, pink-flowered spikes. It grows both in water and on land. Pinkweed, *P. pensylvanicum*, has more slender, lighter-colored spikes.

Deptford Pink, *Dianthus armeria*

Flowers: Several, in terminal clusters, each flower up to ½" across. **Petals:** 5, separated, pink speckled with white. **Stems:** Upright, sparsely branched, finely hairy, up to 1½' tall. **Leaves:** Opposite, simple, linear to linear-lanceolate, without teeth; finely hairy, up to 3" long. **Season:** May–Aug. **Habitat:** Fields, roadsides. **Range** (*see map*): Areas 1–6, 9, 10, E, F. **Family:** Pink. **Comments:** The white-speckled pink petals and narrow, opposite leaves distinguish this species.

▲ Stork's-bill
5 separated petals. 5 stamens.

▲ Flower-of-an-hour
5 separated petals. Many stamens.

▼ Scarlet Smartweed
5 separated petal-like parts.
3-8 stamens.

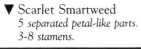

▼ Deptford Pink
5 separated petals. 10 stamens.

RADIAL SYMMETRY

Long-plumed Avens, *Geum triflorum*

Flowers: Solitary, nodding, up to 1″ long. **Petals:** 5, separated, pink or white, but not as conspicuous as the 5 pink sepals. **Stems:** Upright, hairy, up to 2′ tall. **Leaves:** Basal, pinnately divided into fern-like segments, hairy. **Season:** May–July. **Habitat:** Open areas. **Range** (*see map*): Areas 1, 3, 7–10, B–E. **Family:** Rose. **Comments:** The nodding pink flowers and fern-like foliage distinguish this species. Large-leaved avens, *G. macrophyllum*, has yellow flowers and leafy stems; turbinate avens, *G. turbinatum*, has yellow flowers and leafless stems.

Oregon Sidalcea, *Sidalcea oregana*

Flowers: Crowded into terminal spikes, each flower up to 1½″ across. **Petals:** 5, separated, notched at the tip, each on a short stalk. **Stems:** Upright, hairy, up to 5′ tall. **Leaves:** Basal and alternate, simple, hairy; the basal leaves are shallowly palmately 5- or 7-lobed; the upper leaves are more deeply lobed. **Season:** June–Aug. **Habitat:** Dry soil. **Range** (*see map*): Areas 8–10, C. **Family:** Mallow. **Comments:** The cluster of short-stalked flowers distinguishes this handsome wildflower. New Mexico sidalcea, *S. neomexicana*, has conspicuously stalked flowers; checkerbloom, *S. malvaeflora*, has white-veined petals.

Poppy Mallow, *Callirhoe papaver*

Flowers: Few, terminal, up to 2½″ across, each surrounded from below by 3 small, leaf-like structures (bractlets). **Petals:** 5, separated. **Stems:** Upright, hairy, up to 1½′ tall. **Leaves:** Alternate, deeply palmately divided into 5 or 7 generally toothless lobes. **Season:** June–Aug. **Habitat:** Prairies, dry woods. **Range** (*see map*): Areas 2, 3, 5, 6. **Family:** Mallow. **Comments:** This showy species is distinguished by its 3 bractlets and toothless leaf lobes. Winecups, *C. involucrata*, has 3 bractlets and toothed leaf lobes; triangular poppy mallow, *C. triangulata*, has 3 bractlets and triangular, unlobed leaves; palmate poppy mallow, *C. digitata*, lacks bractlets and has smooth sepals; prairie poppy mallow, *C. alcaeoides*, lacks bractlets and has hairy sepals.

Marsh Pink, *Sabatia angularis*

Flowers: Solitary to few, terminal, up to 1½″ across. **Petals:** 5 (rarely 6), barely united at the base. **Stems:** Upright, branched, 4-sided, smooth, up to 2½′ tall. **Leaves:** Opposite, simple, ovate, toothless; smooth, up to 1″ across. **Season:** June–Sept. **Habitat:** Moist, open areas. **Range** (*see map*): Areas 1–3, 5, 6. **Family:** Gentian. **Comments:** The flowers have a delicate fragrance. Prairie sabatia, *S. campestris*, has strictly solitary flowers.

▲ Long-plumed Avens
  5 separated petals. Many stamens.

▲ Oregon Sidalcea
  5 separated petals. Many stamens.

▲ Poppy Mallow
  5 separated petals. Many stamens.

▲ Marsh Pink
  5 (or 6) united petals.

RADIAL SYMMETRY

Capitate Waterleaf, *Hydrophyllum capitatum*

Flowers: Crowded into nearly spherical heads up to 1½" across. **Petals:** 5, united below, up to ½" long. **Stems:** Upright, up to 16" tall. **Leaves:** Alternate and basal, up to 6" long, pinnately divided into 7–11 leaflets that have a few teeth near the tip. **Season:** March–July. **Habitat:** Open areas. **Range** (*see map*): Areas 8–10, C. **Family:** Waterleaf. **Comments:** The leaves of this plant are tender and can be eaten as greens. Pinkish-purple waterleafs in eastern North America that have palmately lobed, maple-like leaves include Canadian waterleaf, *H. canadense*, with usually smooth flower stalks; and appendaged waterleaf, *H. appendiculatum*, with densely hairy flower stalks.

Eastern Phlox, *Phlox divaricata*

Flowers: Several, in terminal clusters, up to 1¼" across. **Petals:** 5, united below into a slender tube, the lobes sometimes notched at the tip. **Stems:** Both creeping and upright, finely hairy, up to 18" tall. **Leaves:** Opposite, simple, lanceolate to oblong, without teeth; finely hairy, up to 4" long. **Season:** April–June. **Habitat:** Rich woods. **Range** (*see map*): Areas 1–6, E. **Family:** Phlox. **Comments:** This wildflower is sometimes called sweet william. Hairy Phlox, *P. pilosa*, is similar but has much hairier stems and leaves; spotted phlox, *P. maculata*, has purple speckles on its stem.

Hairy Phlox, *Phlox pilosa*

Flowers: Several, in terminal clusters, each flower about 1¼" across, on hairy stalks. **Petals:** 5, united below into a slender tube. **Stems:** Upright, sometimes branched, very hairy, up to 1½" tall. **Leaves:** Opposite, simple, very narrow to lanceolate, without teeth; hairy, up to 4" long. **Season:** April–June. **Habitat:** Dry woods, prairies. **Range** (*see map*): Areas 1–6, D, E. **Family:** Phlox. **Comments:** This handsome wildflower is distinguished by its narrow, densely hairy leaves and its upright stature. Eastern phlox, *P. divaricata*, is a similar upright phlox but has broader, less hairy leaves.

Smooth Phlox, *Phlox glaberrima*

Flowers: Several, in terminal clusters, each flower about 1" across. **Petals:** 5, united below into a slender tube. **Stems:** Upright, branched, smooth, up to 2' tall. **Leaves:** Opposite, simple, narrowly lanceolate, without teeth; smooth. **Season:** May–Aug. **Habitat:** Prairies, open woods. **Range** (*see map*): Areas 1–3, 6. **Family:** Phlox. **Comments:** This species is recognized by its smooth narrow leaves. The similar western long-leaved phlox, *P. longifolia*, usually has somewhat hairy leaves and stems; Carolina phlox, *P. carolina*, usually has broader leaves.

▼ Eastern Phlox
  5 united petals. 5 stamens.

▼ Smooth Phlox
  5 united petals. 5 stamens.

▲ Capitate Waterleaf
  5 united petals. 5 stamens.

▲ Hairy Phlox
  5 united petals. 5 stamens.

RADIAL SYMMETRY

Pink Swamp Milkweed, *Asclepias incarnata*

Flowers: Several, arranged in clusters (umbels), each flower about ⅔"
long. **Petals:** 5, pink or pink-red, hanging downward. **Stems:** Upright,
branched, usually hairy, up to 5' tall, with milky sap. **Leaves:** Opposite,
simple, lanceolate, without teeth; usually hairy, up to 3" long, with milky
sap. **Season:** June–Aug. **Habitat:** Swamps, wet ground. **Range** (*see map*):
Areas 1–8, D–F. **Family:** Milkweed. **Comments:** The distinguishing
features of this wetland milkweed are its pink to pink-red flowers about
⅔" long. White swamp milkweed, *A. perennis*, has white flowers about ⅓"
long.

Common Milkweed, *Asclepias syriaca*

Flowers: Several, in large, round-headed clusters (umbels), each flower
up to 1" long. **Petals:** 5, purple or greenish purple, hanging downward.
Stems: Upright, stout, hairy, unbranched, up to 6' tall, with milky sap.
Leaves: Opposite, simple, thick, oblong, without teeth; hairy on the
lower surface, up to 6" long. **Season:** June–Aug. **Habitat:** Fields, prairies,
open areas. **Range** (*see map*): Areas 1–6, D–F. **Family:** Milkweed.
Comments: This species is distinguished by its thick hairy leaves and dull
purple flowers. Very similar is the western milkweed, *A. speciosa*, which
has somewhat larger flowers.

Hairy-fruited Morning Glory, *Ipomoea trichocarpa*

Flowers: 1–2 at the end of a long stalk, up to 2" long. **Petals:** 5, spreading,
sometimes with white lines. **Stems:** Climbing or trailing, up to 3' long.
Leaves: Alternate, often 3-lobed and resembling an ivy leaf; hairy.
Season: June–Oct. **Habitat:** Open areas. **Range** (*see map*): Areas 2, 6.
Family: Morning glory. **Comments:** Other morning glories with lobed
leaves include ivy-leaved morning glory, *I. hederacea*, with leaf lobes more
pointed and flowers 2" long; and Lindheimer's morning glory, *I. lindheimeri*,
with leaves sometimes 5-lobed and with flowers 3"–4" long.

Stalked Wild Petunia, *Ruellia pedunculata*

Flowers: 1–3, arising from the axils of the leaves, each flower up to 2¼"
long. **Petals:** 5, united into a funnel-shaped tube. **Stems:** Upright, usually
branched, minutely hairy, up to 24" tall. **Leaves:** Opposite, simple,
lanceolate, without teeth; usually somewhat hairy, up to 4" long. **Season:**
June–Aug. **Habitat:** Dry woods. **Range** (*see map*): Areas 2, 3, 6. **Family:**
Acanthus. **Comments:** Hairy wild petunia, *R. humilis*, is similar but has
densely hairy stems and leaves.

▼ Common Milkweed
5 united petals. 5 stamens.

▲ Pink Swamp Milkweed
5 united petals. 5 stamens.

▲ Hairy-fruited Morning Glory
5 united petals. 5 stamens.

◀ Stalked Wild Petunia
5 united petals. 5 stamens.

PINK–PURPLE

RADIAL SYMMETRY

Parry's Primrose, *Primula parryi*

Flowers: Up to 12 at the tip of a leafless stalk, each flower ½″–1¼″ across. **Petals:** 5, united at the base into a tube. **Stems:** Upright, up to 16″ long, leafless. **Leaves:** All at the base of the plant, oblong, toothless, up to 12″ long. **Season:** June–Aug. **Habitat:** Wet soil. **Range** (*see map*): Areas 7–9. **Family:** Primrose. **Comments:** The flowers of this plant have the odor of spoiled meat. Narrow-leaved primrose, *P. angustifolia*, has narrowly lanceolate leaves; gray primrose, *P. incana*, has lilac-colored petals that are notched at the tip and leaves white-coated on the lower surface.

BILATERAL SYMMETRY

Crown Vetch, *Coronilla varia*

Flowers: Several, in crowded terminal clusters (umbels), each flower up to ½″ long. **Petals:** 5, arranged to form a typical pea-shaped flower. **Stems:** Spreading, branched, smooth, up to 18″ long. **Leaves:** Alternate, pinnately compound with 11–25 leaflets; the leaflets are oblong, rounded at the tip, without teeth, up to ¾″ long. **Season:** June–Aug. **Habitat:** Along roads. **Range** (*see map*): Areas 1–6, 8, 9, D, E. **Family:** Pea. **Comments:** A native of Europe, the crown vetch has been introduced along highways to prevent soil erosion. Sericea lespedeza, *L. cuneata*, another Old World species planted along highways, has leaves divided into 3 leaflets.

Northern Sweet Vetch, *Hedysarum boreale*

Flowers: Several, in elongated clusters, ½″–¾″ long. **Petals:** 5, arranged to form a typical pea-shaped flower. **Stems:** Several in a cluster, upright, finely hairy, up to 2′ tall. **Leaves:** Alternate, pinnately divided, with 9–21 leaflets; the leaflets are narrowly oblong to elliptic, sparsely hairy, ½″–1″ long. **Season:** June–Aug. **Habitat:** Open areas in mountains. **Range** (*see map*): Areas 1, 4–9, A–F. **Family:** Pea. **Comments:** The thick roots are edible. The fruiting segments of this species are unwinged. The very similar western sweet vetch, *H. occidentale*, has winged fruiting segments; sulphur sweet vetch, *H. sulphurescens*, has yellow flowers.

Ground Plum, *Astragalus crassicarpus*

Flowers: Several, crowded into short, terminal clusters (racemes), each flower about 1″ long, curved. **Stems:** Upright, hairy, up to 15″ tall. **Leaves:** Alternate, pinnately compound, with 15–23 elliptic, toothless leaflets. **Season:** April–June. **Habitat:** Prairies, plains. **Range** (*see map*): Areas 2–9, C, D. **Family:** Pea. **Comments:** This is one of the largest genera in North America, with nearly 350 species recognized. Many of them are difficult to distinguish. Several species are poisonous.

▲ Parry's Primrose
  5 united petals. 5 stamens.

▲ Crown Vetch
  5 separated petals.
  Pea-shaped flower. 10 stamens.

▼ Northern Sweet Vetch
  5 separated petals.
  Pea-shaped flower. 10 stamens.

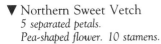

▲ Ground Plum
  5 separated petals.
  Pea-shaped flower. 10 stamens.

BILATERAL SYMMETRY

American Vetch, *Vicia americana*

Flowers: 2–9 in clusters on long stalks arising from the leaf axils, each flower ¾″–1¼″ long. **Petals:** 5, arranged to form a typical pea-shaped flower. **Stems:** Trailing or climbing by coiled tendrils, usually smooth, up to 3′ long. **Leaves:** Alternate, pinnately compound, with 8–14 leaflets; each leaflet is narrowly elliptic, smooth, usually without teeth, ⅔″–1⅓″ long. **Season:** May–July. **Habitat:** Moist woods, sometimes in the mountains. **Range** (*see map*): All areas except 2 and F. **Family:** Pea. **Comments:** Of the 30 different kinds of vetch in North America, several have been introduced from Europe for forage for livestock. Spring vetch, *V. sativa*, is an introduced species with 1 or 2 flowers in a cluster.

Alfalfa, *Medicago sativa*

Flowers: Few, in short clusters on stalks arising from the leaf axils, each flower ⅓″–½″ long. **Petals:** 5, arranged to form a typical pea-shaped flower. **Stems:** Spreading or ascending, smooth or nearly so, up to 3′ long. **Leaves:** Alternate, divided into 3 leaflets; the leaflets are notched and broadest at the tip, smooth, toothed, ⅔″–1⅓″ long. **Season:** June–Sept. **Habitat:** Along roads. **Range** (*see map*): All areas. **Family:** Pea. **Comments:** Alfalfa was introduced from Europe because it is an excellent forage plant for livestock. It makes excellent hay.

Red Clover, *Trifolium pratense*

Flowers: Many, crowded together into a nearly spherical head, each flower about ½″ long. **Petals:** 5, arranged to form a typical pea-shaped flower. **Stems:** Spreading or upright, hairy, up to 2′ long. **Leaves:** Alternate, divided into 3 leaflets; each leaflet is oval, finely toothed, hairy, up to 2″ long. **Season:** May–Sept. **Habitat:** Open, disturbed soil; in old fields; along roads. **Range** (*see map*): All areas. **Family:** Pea. **Comments:** The flowers of red clover are actually pink. This is an excellent forage plant for livestock and was introduced from Europe for that purpose. Native pink- or purple-flowered clovers found in woods, on prairies, or in dry fields include Carolina clover, *T. carolinianum*, with flowers up to ⅓″ long; and buffalo clover, *T. reflexum*, with flowers ⅓″–½″ long.

Prairie Spider-flower, *Cleome serrulata*

Flowers: Several, in terminal clusters, up to 1½″ wide. **Petals:** 4, tapering to a narrow "stalk," all on one side of the flower, about ½″ long. **Stems:** Upright, smooth, to 2½′ tall. **Leaves:** Alternate, divided into 3 leaflets; each leaflet is narrowly lanceolate, without teeth, up to 2½″ long. **Season:** July–Aug. **Habitat:** Prairies. **Range** (*see map*): Areas 3–10, C–E. **Family:** Caper. **Comments:** A frequently planted ornamental is the garden spider-flower, *C. hassleriana*, which has larger flowers, hairy stems, and leaves divided into 5 or 7 leaflets.

▲ American Vetch
  5 separated petals.
  Pea-shaped flower. 10 stamens.

◀ Alfalfa
  5 separated petals.
  Pea-shaped flower. 10 stamens.

▼ Prairie Spider-flower
  4 separated petals. 6 stamens.

▼ Red Clover
  5 separated petals.
  Pea-shaped flower. 10 stamens.

BILATERAL SYMMETRY

Scarlet Beeblossom, *Gaura coccinea*

Flowers: Several, but not crowded, in a terminal cluster, each flower up to 1″ across. **Petals:** 4, arranged on one side of the flower, up to ⅓″ long. **Stems:** Upright, much branched, up to 3′ tall. **Leaves:** Alternate, simple, narrowly elliptic, usually toothed; up to 3″ long. **Season:** March–Sept. **Habitat:** Sandy soil. **Range** (*see map*): Areas 3–10, C–E. **Family:** Evening Primrose. **Comments:** Other gauras common in North America include small-flowered beeblossom, *G. parviflora*, with pink petals about ⅒″ long; and long-flowered beeblossom, *G. longiflora*, with petals ¼″–½″ long and lanceolate leaves.

Calypso Orchid, *Calypso bulbosa*

Flowers: Solitary, at the tip of a leafless stalk, 1″–1¼″ long. **Petal-like Parts:** 6; 5 are rose-pink and 1—the lip—is white with purplish spots and has two short horns at the tip. **Stems:** Upright, smooth, leafless, bearing the flower, up to 8″ tall. **Leaf:** 1 basal leaf, spherical but with a distinct stalk, smooth, up to 2½″ long. **Season:** June–Aug. **Habitat:** Rich woods, shaded areas. **Range** (*see map*): Areas 1, 3, 4, 7–10, A–F. **Family:** Orchid. **Comments:** A similar rose-pink orchid with a single, basal, narrower leaf and a solitary flower with a fringed lip petal is rose pogonia, *Pogonia ophioglossoides*. Grass-pink orchid, *Calopogon tuberosus*, has several similar flowers and several long, narrow leaves.

Spotted Coral-root Orchid, *Corallorhiza maculata*

Flowers: Several, in an elongated cluster, each flower ¾″ across. **Petal-like Parts:** 6; 5 are pink and 1—the lip—is broader, white with purple spots. **Stems:** Upright, pink to brown, up to 30″ tall. **Leaves:** None, or reduced to non-green sheaths. **Season:** April–Sept. **Habitat:** Rich woods, shaded areas. **Range** (*see map*): Areas 1–3, 5-10, C–F. **Family:** Orchid. **Comments:** All coral-roots lack green leaves and stems and rely on organic matter in the soil for their nutrition. Striped coral-root orchid, *C. striata*, has petal-like parts with parallel purple-brown stripes; pale coral-root, *C. trifida*, has smaller flowers less than ½″ across.

Pink Milkwort, *Polygala sanguinea*

Flowers: Several, crowded into a short-cylindrical head about ½″ thick. **Petals:** Have the appearance of 5, not all alike, usually pink but sometimes green or white. **Stems:** Upright, smooth, up to 15″ tall. **Leaves:** Alternate, simple, very narrow, without teeth; smooth, 1¼″ long. **Season:** July–Sept. **Habitat:** Old fields, open woods. **Range** (*see map*): Areas 1–7, E, F. **Family:** Milkwort. **Comments:** Whorled milkwort, *P. cruciata*, has similar flower heads, but the leaves are in whorls of four.

▲ Scarlet Beeblossom
   4 separated petals. 8 stamens.

▼ Spotted Coral-root Orchid
   Separated petal-like parts.
   1 stamen.

▼ Calypso Orchid
   Separated petal-like parts. 1 stamen.

▼ Pink Milkwort
   5 united petals and petal-like parts.
   6 or 8 stamens.

BILATERAL SYMMETRY

Lemon Beebalm, *Monarda citriodora*

Flowers: Clustered in rings along the upper part of the stem, each ring with a pair of pale yellow or pink leaves at its base. **Petals:** 5, dotted with dark pink, forming 2 lips, up to 1″ long. **Stems:** Upright, finely hairy, up to 2½′ tall. **Leaves:** Opposite, simple, lanceolate or oblong, usually toothed; finely hairy, up to 2½″ long. **Season:** April–Oct. **Habitat:** Rocky soil, prairies, meadows. **Range** (*see map*): Areas 2, 3, 5–7. **Family:** Mint. **Comments:** Other beebalms with flowers in several rings include the plains beebalm, M. *pectinata*, with green leaves below each group of flowers; and spotted beebalm, M. *punctata*, with white or yellowish leaves below each group of flowers and with white or yellow petals spotted with maroon.

Wild Bergamot, *Monarda fistulosa*

Flowers: Several, crowded into heads up to 1½″ across, each flower up to 1½″ long. **Petals:** 5, united below, 2-lipped. **Stems:** Upright, usually branched, hairy, to 2½′ tall. **Leaves:** Opposite, simple, lanceolate, toothed; up to 4″ long. **Season:** June–Sept. **Habitat:** Woods, prairies. **Range** (*see map*): Areas 1–9, C–E. **Family:** Mint. **Comments:** Horsemint, M. *bradburiana*, is similar but has leaves without stalks.

Unicorn Plant, *Martynia proboscidea*

Flowers: Few, in an elongated terminal cluster, each flower up to 2″ across. **Petals:** 5, united below, 2-lipped, up to 2″ long. **Stems:** Upright, with sticky hairs, up to 3′ tall. **Leaves:** Opposite, simple, nearly spherical, heart-shaped at the base, without teeth; with sticky hairs, up to 9″ across. **Season:** May–Sept. **Habitat:** Open areas. **Range** (*see map*): Areas 1-10, D, E. **Family:** Martynia. **Comments:** The unusual fruit is a capsule with a hard, upwardly curved, hooked horn. Golden devil's claw, M. *althaeifolia*, has bright yellow flowers.

Self-heal, *Prunella vulgaris*

Flowers: Several, crowded together into terminal spikes and spikes in the leaf axils, each flower up to ½″ long. **Petals:** 5, united, 2-lipped, the lower lip fringed. **Stems:** Upright or creeping, hairy, up to 18″ long. **Leaves:** Opposite, simple, oblong to ovate, toothed; hairy. **Season:** May–Sept. **Habitat:** Lawns, fields, roadsides. **Range** (*see map*): Areas 1-10, C–F. **Family:** Mint. **Comments:** There is variation in leaf shape and degree of hairiness and in whether the plants are erect or creeping.

Wild Bergamot ▶
5 united petals. 2 stamens.

▼ Unicorn Plant
5 united petals. 4 stamens.

▲ Lemon Beebalm
5 united petals. 2 stamens.

Self-heal ▶
5 united petals. 4 stamens.

BILATERAL SYMMETRY

Blue Monkey-flower, *Mimulus alatus*

Flowers: Solitary, in the leaf axils, 1″–1½″ long. **Petals:** 5, united, 2-lipped. **Stems:** Upright, square, smooth, up to 3′ tall. **Leaves:** Opposite, simple, lanceolate to ovate, toothed; smooth, with stalks. **Season:** July–Sept. **Habitat:** Wet soil, often in woods. **Range** (*see map*): Areas 1–3, 5, 6, E. **Family:** Snapdragon. **Comments:** Another blue monkey-flower, *M. ringens*, differs by having leaves without stalks. The pygmy monkey-flower, *M. rubellus*, a species of deserts, has red flowers only ¼″ long.

Owl's Clover, *Orthocarpus purpurascens*

Flowers: Crowded into dense terminal clusters, each flower 1″–1¼″ long. **Petals:** 5, united, 2-lipped. **Stems:** Upright, hairy, up to 15″ tall. **Leaves:** Alternate, deeply divided into several long and very narrow leaflets; hairy, up to 2″ long. **Season:** April–May. **Habitat:** Fields, woods, open areas. **Range** (*see map*): Areas 7, 9, 10, C. **Family:** Snapdragon. **Comments:** Yellow owl's clover, *O. luteus*, has golden yellow flowers ⅓″–½″ long; hairy owl's clover, *O. hispidus*, has pale yellow flowers ½″–⅔″ long.

Elephant Heads, *Pedicularis groenlandica*

Flowers: Crowded into elongated terminal clusters, each flower ½″–¾″ long. **Petals:** 5, united, 2-lipped, the upper lip resembling an elephant's trunk, the lower lip forming the elephant's ears. **Stems:** Upright, smooth, up to 2½′ tall. **Leaves:** Alternate, deeply divided into more than 20 lobes; smooth, up to 10″ long. **Season:** June–Aug. **Habitat:** Wet soil, often in meadows. **Range** (*see map*): Areas 7–10, A–E. **Family:** Snapdragon. **Comments:** Parrot's-beak, *P. racemosa*, has pale pink flowers, the upper petals curved like a parrot's beak, and undivided leaves; lousewort, *P. canadensis*, has yellow flowers and deeply lobed leaves.

Purple Dead Nettle, *Lamium purpureum*

Flowers: Several, in dense clusters, each flower up to ½″ long. **Petals:** 5, united, 2-lipped. **Stems:** Upright or spreading, branched, hairy, up to 15″ long. **Leaves:** Opposite, simple, ovate, heart-shaped at base; hairy, all on stalks. **Season:** April–Oct. **Habitat:** Disturbed soil. **Range** (*see map*): All areas except 4, 7, B, D. **Family:** Mint. **Comments:** Henbit, *L. amplexicaule*, is similar, but the upper leaves lack stalks.

▲ Blue Monkey-flower
5 united petals. 4 stamens.

Owl's Clover ▶
5 united petals. 4 stamens.

▼ Elephant Heads
5 united petals. 4 stamens.

▼ Purple Dead Nettle
5 united petals. 4 stamens.

BILATERAL SYMMETRY

Nettleleaf Horsemint, *Agastache urticifolia*

Flowers: Crowded into a terminal cluster up to 6″ long, each flower about ½″ long. **Petals:** 5, united, 2-lipped. **Stems:** Upright, smooth, up to 5′ tall. **Leaves:** Opposite, simple, ovate, toothed; nearly smooth, up to 3″ long. **Season:** June–Aug. **Habitat:** Open woods. **Range** (*see map*): Areas 8–10, C. **Family:** Mint. **Comments:** Other members of this genus include the purple giant hyssop, *A. scrophulariaefolia*, with purple petals and usually a hairy stem; yellow giant hyssop, *A. nepetoides*, with yellow petals; and blue giant hyssop, *A. foeniculum*, with blue petals.

Pink Plains Penstemon, *Penstemon ambiguus*

Flowers: Several, but not crowded, in a terminal cluster, each flower up to 1½″ long. **Petals:** 5, united, 2-lipped. **Stems:** Upright, smooth or hairy, up to 4½′ tall. **Leaves:** Opposite, simple, very narrow, without teeth; up to 2″ long. **Season:** May–Aug. **Habitat:** Open, often sandy areas. **Range** (*see map*): Areas 5–8. **Family:** Snapdragon. **Comments:** The flowers of this species are sometimes white. There are about 230 penstemons native to North America, the majority of them found in the West. Slender penstemon, *P. tenuis*, another pink-flowered species, has toothed leaves ¾″–1¼″ wide.

Foxglove Penstemon, *Penstemon cobaea*

Flowers: Several, but not crowded, in a terminal cluster, each flower 1½″–3″ long. **Petals:** 5, united below into an inflated tube, 2-lipped. **Stems:** Upright, hairy, up to 2′ tall. **Leaves:** Opposite, simple, broadly elliptic, toothed; hairy, up to 3½″ long. **Season:** April-June. **Habitat:** Prairies. **Range** (*see map*): Areas 2, 3, 5–7. **Family:** Snapdragon. **Comments:** The flowers are among the largest in the genus. Nearly as large are the pale purple flowers of the large-flowered penstemon, *P. grandiflorus*, which also has smooth, toothless leaves.

Palmer's Penstemon, *Penstemon palmeri*

Flowers: Several, but not crowded, in an elongated terminal cluster, each flower up to 1½″ long. **Petals:** 5, united below into an inflated tube, 2-lipped. **Stems:** Upright, up to 5½′ tall. **Leaves:** Opposite, simple, lanceolate, without teeth; blue-green, up to 10″ long, without a stalk. **Season:** March–Sept. **Habitat:** Rocky soil. **Range** (*see map*): Areas 7, 8, 10. **Family:** Snapdragon. **Comments:** Virgate penstemon, *P. virgatus*, is a similar species with very narrow leaves.

▲ Nettleleaf Horsemint
  5 united petals. 4 stamens.

▲ Pink Plains Penstemon
  5 united petals. 4 stamens.

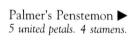

Palmer's Penstemon ▶
  5 united petals. 4 stamens.

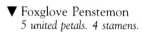

▼ Foxglove Penstemon
  5 united petals. 4 stamens.

RED–ORANGE

ASTER FAMILY

Blanket Flower, *Gaillardia pulchella*

Flowers: Crowded into daisy-like heads up to 2″ across. Ray flowers number 40 or more, tipped with yellow, with 3 teeth at tip, up to ¾″ long. Disk flowers are tubular, 5-lobed, purple-red. **Stems:** Upright, branched, hairy, up to 2′ tall. **Leaves:** Alternate, simple, oblong, the lower toothed, the upper often without teeth; hairy, up to 3″ long. **Season:** May–July. **Habitat:** Open, often sandy soil. **Range** (*see map*): Areas 1–8, 10. **Family:** Aster. **Comments:** Other gaillardias include the red-domed blanket flower, *G. pinnatifida*, with yellow rays, a red-domed disk, and deeply lobed leaves; plains blanket flower, *G. aristata*, with yellow rays, a nearly flat red-purple disk, and deeply lobed leaves; and lance-leaved blanket flower, *G. lanceolata*, with yellow rays and a yellow disk.

King Devil, *Hieracium aurantiacum*

Flowers: Crowded into dandelion-like heads up to 1″ across, usually several heads together. Ray flowers are orange, up to ⅔″ long, minutely toothed at the tip. No disk flowers. **Stems:** Upright, with few alternate, simple leaves, or without leaves; densely hairy, up to 2′ tall. **Leaves:** Mostly clustered at base of plant, elliptic or slightly broadest above the middle, usually without teeth; densely hairy, up to 8″ long. **Season:** June–Sept. **Habitat:** Fields, roadsides, disturbed areas. **Range** (*see map*): Areas 1–3, 9, 10, A, C–F. **Family:** Aster. **Comments:** Most of the other 45 members of this genus in North America are yellow-flowered. These include slender hawkweed, *H. gracile*, with nearly smooth leaves less than 3″ long; umbellate hawkweed, *H. umbellatum*, with hairy, toothed leaves up to 5″ long; and rough hawkweed, *H. scabrum*, with hairy, usually toothless leaves up to 8″ long.

RADIAL SYMMETRY

Turk's-cap Lily, *Lilium michiganense*

Flowers: 1 to several, nodding, up to 6″ long. **Petal-like Parts:** Orange or orange-red, spotted with purple, strongly curved backward. **Stems:** Upright, smooth, to 6′ tall. **Leaves:** Whorled, simple, without teeth; smooth, up to 5″ long. **Season:** May–July. **Habitat:** Moist woods, prairies. **Range** (*see map*): Areas 1–5, E. **Family:** Lily. **Comments:** Canada lily, *L. canadense*, has nodding flowers with petal-like parts that are not strongly curved backward; wood lily, *L. philadelphicum*, has erect flowers.

Orange Day Lily, *Hemerocallis fulva*

Flowers: Several, erect, up to 6″ long. **Petal-like Parts:** 6, united below into a tube. **Stems:** Upright, smooth, up to 6′ tall. **Leaves:** All basal, elongated, pointed at the tip, without teeth; smooth, up to ½″ across. **Season:** June–Aug. **Habitat:** Roadsides; open, disturbed areas. **Range** (*see map*): Areas 1–6, 8, E, F. **Family:** Lily. **Comments:** This native of the Old World is commonly planted in gardens and frequently found along country roads.

◀ Blanket Flower
Ray and disk flowers.

▼ Turk's-cap Lily
6 petal-like parts.

▲ King Devil
Ray flowers only. Milky sap.

▼ Orange Day Lily
6 petal-like parts.

RADIAL SYMMETRY

Firepink, *Silene virginica*

Flowers: Several, in a branched, terminal cluster, each flower up to 1½″ across. **Petals:** 5, deeply notched at tip, up to 1½″ long. **Stems:** Upright, branched, sticky-hairy, up to 2′ tall. **Leaves:** Opposite, simple, lanceolate, without teeth; hairy, up to 4″ long. **Season:** April–May. **Habitat:** Moist or dry woods. **Range** (*see map*): Areas 1–3, 6, E. **Family:** Pink. **Comments:** Moss catchfly, *S. acaulis*, is a pink-flowered, mat-forming species found in alpine areas.

Mexican Campion, *Silene laciniata*

Flowers: 1–3, terminal, up to 1″ across. **Petals:** Deeply 5-cleft, with narrow, pointed divisions. **Stems:** Upright, branched, finely hairy, up to 2′ tall. **Leaves:** Opposite, simple, lanceolate, without teeth; finely hairy, up to 6″ long. **Season:** April–Oct. **Habitat:** Dry woods, often in mountains. **Range** (*see map*): Areas 6, 7, 10. **Family:** Pink. **Comments:** This is one of the showiest wildflowers in North America. California campion, *S. californica*, is similar, but the petal divisions are less pointed and the leaves broader.

Wild Columbine, *Aquilegia canadensis*

Flowers: Several, nodding from the ends of the branches, up to 2½″ long. **Petals:** 5, projected backward into 5 hollow spurs 1″ long, red on the outside, yellow inside. **Stems:** Upright, branched, up to 3′ tall. **Leaves:** Basal and alternate, divided into round-lobed segments. **Season:** April–June. **Habitat:** Rocky woods. **Range** (*see map*): Areas 1–5, D–F. **Family:** Buttercup. **Comments:** The ends of the hollow spurs contain nectar. Similar species include crimson columbine, *A. formosa*, which grows 2′–3½′ tall and has yellow petals with crimson spurs less than 1″ long; and elegant columbine, *A. elegantula*, which grows only up to 1½′ tall and has yellow petals with crimson spurs less than 1″ long.

California Poppy, *Eschscholtzia californica*

Flowers: Solitary, on a long stalk, up to 2″ across. **Petals:** Broad and rounded at tip, tapering to base. **Stems:** Upright, up to 21″ tall, bearing the solitary flower. **Leaves:** All basal, deeply divided and fern-like; blue-green, up to 2½″ long. **Season:** Feb–Sept. **Habitat:** Open areas. **Range** (*see map*): Areas 8–10, C, D, F. **Family:** Poppy. **Comments:** This is the state flower of California. Its flowers open only during the day. Gold poppy, *E. mexicana*, has slightly smaller, usually yellow flowers.

▲ Firepink
  5 separated petals.

◀ Mexican Campion
  5 separated petals.

▼ California Poppy
  4 separated petals. Many stamens.

▼ Wild Columbine
  5 separated petals. Many stamens.

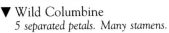

RED–ORANGE

RADIAL SYMMETRY

Desert Globe Mallow, *Sphaeralcea ambigua*

Flowers: Several, not crowded, in an elongated terminal cluster, each flower up to 1½" across. **Petals:** Orange-red, round-tipped. **Stems:** Upright, hairy, up to 8' tall. **Leaves:** Alternate, simple; with 3 broad, shallow, toothed lobes; hairy, up to 2½" long. **Season:** Jan–Dec. **Habitat:** Deserts. **Range** (*see map*): Areas 7, 8, 10. **Family:** Mallow. **Comments:** The petals of this species are sometimes pink-purple. Scarlet globe mallow, *S. coccinea,* is similar but has deeply palmately lobed, gray-hairy leaves.

Narrow-leaved Globe Mallow, *Sphaeralcea angustifolia*

Flowers: Several, not crowded, in an elongated terminal cluster, each flower up to 1½" across. **Petals:** Orange-red, sometimes pink, round-tipped. **Stems:** Upright, hairy, up to 4½' tall. **Leaves:** Alternate, simple, lanceolate, usually toothed; hairy, up to 4" long. **Season:** Jan–Dec. **Habitat:** Sandy or rocky soil. **Range** (*see map*): Areas 5–8, 10. **Family:** Mallow. **Comments:** Wrinkled globe mallow, *S. subhastata,* is very similar, but the leaves usually have a pair of very shallow lobes near the base.

Red Claret Cactus, *Echinocereus triglochidiatus*

Flowers: Solitary, up to 2½" across. **Petal-like Parts:** Numerous, separated. **Stems:** Cylindrical, up to 3" in diameter, growing in clumps, with 0–4 central spines and 4–12 radial spines per central area (areole). **Season:** April–July. **Habitat:** Deserts, rocky woods. **Range** (*see map*): Areas 6–8, 10. **Family:** Cactus. **Comments:** There are several variations of this cactus based upon the number of central and radial spines per areole. There are more than a dozen species of *Echinocereus* in the western United States. Most of them are called hedgehog cactus.

BILATERAL SYMMETRY

Spotted Touch-me-not, *Impatiens capensis*

Flowers: 1–3 on slender drooping stalks arising from the leaf axils, up to 1½" long. **Petal-like Parts:** Have appearance of 6, of different shapes and sizes, one of them prolonged backward into a spur. **Stems:** Upright, branched, smooth, up to 5' tall. **Leaves:** Alternate, simple, elliptic to ovate, toothed; smooth, up to 4½" long. **Season:** June–Sept. **Habitat:** Wet soil, moist woods. **Range** (*see map*): All areas except 7 and 10. **Family:** Jewelweed. **Comments:** When the seeds are mature, they explode from their capsule at the slightest touch. The juice from the stem sometimes gives relief from poison ivy rash. Pale touch-me-not, *I. pallida,* has nearly identical leaves and yellow flowers.

▲ Desert Globe Mallow
5 separated petals.
Many stamens.

▲ Narrow-leaved Globe Mallow
5 separated petals.
Many stamens.

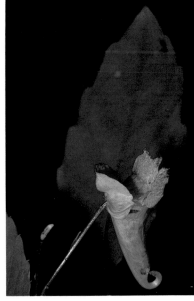

▲ Red Claret Cactus
Many separated petals.
Many stamens.

▲ Spotted Touch-me-not
Dissimilar petal-like parts
(have appearance of 6).

RADIAL SYMMETRY

Indian Pink, *Spigelia marilandica*

Flowers: Several, usually formed along one side of a terminal stalk, each flower up to 2″ long. **Petals:** 5, united to form a slender tube, red on the outside, yellow on the inside. **Stems:** Upright, unbranched, smooth, up to 2′ tall. **Leaves:** Opposite, simple, ovate, toothless; smooth, up to 3½″ long, without a stalk. **Season:** May–Oct. **Habitat:** Rich woods. **Range** (*see map*): Areas 1–3, 6. **Family:** Logania. **Comments:** 4 or 5 other species of *Spigelia* are restricted to southern Texas or peninsular Florida.

Butterfly-weed, *Asclepias tuberosa*

Flowers: Several, in umbrella-like clusters, each flower up to ½″ long. **Petals:** 5, projecting downward. **Stems:** Upright, hairy, up to 2½′ tall without milky sap. **Leaves:** Alternate or mixed with some opposite leaves, without teeth; hairy, up to 3″ long. **Season:** April–Sept. **Habitat:** Prairies, fields, open woods. **Range** (*see map*): Areas 1–8, E. **Family:** Milkweed. **Comments:** Other showy red- and yellow-flowered milkweeds are Mexican milkweed, *A. curassavica*, with hairy opposite leaves and milky sap; and lance-leaved milkweed, *A. lanceolata*, with smooth opposite leaves and milky sap.

BILATERAL SYMMETRY

Crimson Clover, *Trifolium incarnatum*

Flowers: Many, crowded together into cylindrical spikes up to 2½″ long, each flower ½″–⅔″ long. **Petals:** Arranged to form a typical pea-shaped flower. **Stems:** Upright, hairy, up to 2½′ tall. **Leaves:** Alternate, divided into 3 leaflets, the leaflets broadest above the middle, tapering to the base, minutely toothed; hairy, up to 1½″ long. **Season:** May–Aug. **Habitat:** Roadsides. **Range** (*see map*): Areas 1–6, 9, 10, C, E. **Family:** Pea. **Comments:** This handsome clover is a native of Europe and was planted in this country for its forage value for livestock.

Cardinal Flower, *Lobelia cardinalis*

Flowers: Several, scattered in an elongated, terminal cluster, each flower up to 2″ long. **Petals:** United but split to the base on one side, forming 2 lips. **Stems:** Upright, smooth or hairy, usually unbranched, up to 4½′ tall. **Leaves:** Alternate, simple, lanceolate or oblong, finely toothed; smooth or hairy, up to 6″ long. **Season:** July–Sept. **Habitat:** Wet ground. **Range** (*see map*): Areas 1–3, 5, 6, 8, 10, E, F. **Family:** Harebell. **Comments:** This is one of the most handsome of all North American wildflowers. A very similar species but with narrower leaves is splendid lobelia, *L. splendens*.

▲ Indian Pink
  5 united petals.

Butterfly-weed ▶
5 united petals.

▼ Crimson Clover
  *Separated petal-like parts
  (have appearance of 4).*

▼ Cardinal Flower
  5 united petals.

BILATERAL SYMMETRY

Trumpet Bouvardia, *Bouvardia ternifolia*

Flowers: Few, in elongated terminal clusters, each flower up to 1½" long. **Petals:** 4, not all the same size, united to form a slender tube. **Stems:** Upright, sometimes branched, smooth or hairy, up to 3' tall. **Leaves:** Simple, usually in groups of 3, lanceolate to ovate, without teeth; smooth or hairy, up to 2" long. **Season:** July–Sept. **Habitat:** Rocky woods. **Range** (*see map*): Areas 6 and 7. **Family:** Madder. **Comments:** This showy plant differs from others with red, tubular flowers by its leaves in groups of 3.

Desert Paintbrush, *Castilleja chromosa*

Flowers: Several, crowded at the upper end of the plant, each flower up to 1½" long; surrounding each flower are leaf-like structures (bracts) that are tipped with bright orange-red. **Stems:** Upright, hairy, up to 1½' tall. **Leaves:** Alternate, simple but often with 3 or 5 deep, narrow lobes; up to 2½" long. **Season:** March–Aug. **Habitat:** Dry soil. **Range** (*see map*): Areas 4, 7–10. **Family:** Snapdragon. **Comments:** About 125 different kinds of paintbrushes grow in the West. Some of the other red-flowered ones that usually have some leaves with 3 or 5 lobes are longbill paintbrush, C, *sessiliflora*, which blooms from March to May; and patriotic paintbrush, C. *patriotica*, which blooms from July to September.

Southwestern Paintbrush, *Castilleja integra*

Flowers: Several, crowded into terminal heads, each flower up to 2" long; surrounding each flower are unlobed or 3-lobed leaf-like structures (bracts) that are usually tipped with red. **Stems:** Upright, hairy, up to 28" tall. **Leaves:** Alternate, simple, narrowly lanceolate, toothless and unlobed; hairy, up to 2½" long. **Season:** March–Oct. **Habitat:** Dry soil. **Range** (*see map*): Areas 6–8. **Family:** Snapdragon. **Comments:** Texas paintbrush, C. *indivisa*, has upper leaves usually pinnately lobed; woolly paintbrush, C. *lanata*, has very narrow, white-woolly leaves.

Texas Paintbrush, *Castilleja indivisa*

Flowers: Several, crowded into terminal spikes, each flower surrounded from below by bright red leaf-like structures (bracts). **Petals:** 5, united into a narrow tube, not showy like the bracts. **Stems:** Upright, unbranched, hairy, up to 15" tall. **Leaves:** Alternate, simple, often lobed; hairy. **Season:** March–June. **Habitat:** Roadsides, damp soil. **Range** (*see map*): Areas 2, 6. **Family:** Snapdragon. **Comments:** This is one of the brightest paintbrushes in North America. The combination of vivid red bracts and leaves often lobed distinguishes this species.

▲ Trumpet Bouvardia
   4 united petals.

▲ Desert Paintbrush
   5 united petals.

▼ Southwestern Paintbrush
   5 united petals.

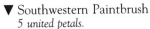

▼ Texas Paintbrush
   5 united petals.

RED–ORANGE

BILATERAL SYMMETRY

Hummingbird Trumpet, *Epilobium canum*

Flowers: Several, in an elongated, terminal cluster, each flower up to 2″ long. **Petals:** 4, notched, united into a long tube. **Stems:** Upright, hairy, up to 2′ tall. **Leaves:** Alternate, simple, elliptic to ovate, toothed; hairy, up to 1¾″ long. **Season:** June–Nov. **Habitat:** Rocky areas. **Range** (*see map*): Areas 7–10. **Family:** Evening Primrose. **Comments:** This showy wildflower is sometimes known by the genus name *Zauschneria*.

Scarlet Penstemon, *Penstemon barbatus*

Flowers: Several, but not crowded, in terminal clusters, each flower up to 1½″ long. **Petals:** Forming 2 lips, the upper lip projecting forward and with 2 pointed teeth, the lower lip turned backward. **Stems:** Upright, usually smooth, up to 4½′ tall. **Leaves:** Opposite, simple, narrowly lanceolate, without teeth; smooth, up to 4″ long. **Season:** June–Oct. **Habitat:** Mountain woods. **Range** (*see map*): Areas 5–8. **Family:** Snapdragon. **Comments:** Bridges' penstemon, *P. bridgesii*, has rounded teeth on the upper lip of the flower.

Scarlet Bugler, *Penstemon centranthifolius*

Flowers: Several, but not crowded, in terminal clusters, each flower up to 1¼″ long. **Petals:** 5, slightly different in size but barely 2-lipped, united below into a long tube. **Stems:** Upright, smooth, up to 4′ tall. **Leaves:** Opposite, simple, lanceolate but rounded at the tip; smooth, up to 3″ long. **Season:** April–July. **Habitat:** Dry soil. **Range** (*see map*): Area 10. **Family:** Snapdragon. **Comments:** Eaton's firecracker, *P. eatonii*, is similar but has pointed leaves.

Parry's Penstemon, *Penstemon parryi*

Flowers: Several, but not crowded, in terminal clusters, each flower up to ¾″ long. **Petals:** 5, somewhat different in size and slightly 2-lipped, united below into a swollen tube. **Stems:** Upright, smooth, up to 4′ tall. **Leaves:** Opposite, simple, lanceolate, without teeth; smooth, blue-green, up to 5″ long. **Season:** Feb–May. **Habitat:** Dry, open areas. **Range** (*see map*): Area 7. **Family:** Snapdragon. **Comments:** Murray's penstemon, *P. murrayanus*, which also has red flowers, has broadly ovate, blue-green leaves.

▲ Hummingbird Trumpet
4 *united petals.*

▲ Scarlet Penstemon
5 *united petals.*

▲ Scarlet Bugler
5 *united petals.*

▲ Parry's Penstemon
5 *united petals.*

ASTER FAMILY

Prairie Dock, *Silphium terebinthinaceum*

Flowers: Crowded together into heads up to 3″ across. Ray flowers are yellow, notched at tip, usually 25 or more in number. Disk flowers are yellow, tubular. **Stems:** Upright, smooth or nearly so, to 10′ tall. **Leaves:** Nearly all basal, simple, broadly ovate, pointed at the tip, heart-shaped at the base, toothed; rough to the touch, up to 8″ across. **Season:** July–Sept. **Habitat:** Prairies, glades. **Range** (*see map*): Areas 1–3, E. **Family:** Aster. **Comments:** This characteristic plant of the prairies is recognized by its large basal leaves with rough hairs. Similar to it, and in similar habitats, is the compass plant, *S. laciniatum*, which has deeply divided leaves.

Goldenweed, *Haplopappus acaulis*

Flowers: Crowded together into heads up to 1½″ across. Ray flowers are yellow, 6–15 per head, about ½″ long. Disk flowers are yellow, tubular. **Stems:** Upright, up to 6″ tall, bearing the flowering heads. **Leaves:** Mostly basal, up to 1½″ long, about ⅓″ wide, with 3 prominent veins. **Season:** May–Aug. **Habitat:** Dry, open areas. **Range** (*see map*): Areas 7–10. **Family:** Aster. **Comments:** This species is distinguished by its short and very narrow leaves, nearly all clustered at the base of the plant. Western goldenweed, *H. armerioides*, is similar, but the stems are usually at least 6″ long and the leaves more than 1½″ long.

Woolly Flower, *Psilostrophe tagetina*

Flowers: Crowded into many densely woolly heads about 1½″ across and on stalks more than ¼″ long. Ray flowers usually number 3, yellow, with 3 notches at the tip of each. Disk flowers are yellow, tubular. **Stems:** Upright, hairy, to 18″ tall. **Leaves:** Basal leaves are ovate, with or without lobes, hairy, up to 3″ long; stem leaves are alternate, narrower and smaller. **Season:** March–Oct. **Habitat:** Open areas, roadsides. **Range** (*see map*): Areas 6–8. **Family:** Aster. **Comments:** Other species of *Psilostrophe* are known as paper flowers. They include *P. gnaphalodes*, with flower heads on stalks less than ¼″ long; and *P. villosa*, with numerous long white hairs on the stem and ray flowers that are more deeply notched.

Arrowleaf Balsamroot, *Balsamorhiza sagittata*

Flowers: Crowded together into heads up to 5″ across. Ray flowers number 8–25, yellow, pointed, up to nearly 2″ long. Disk flowers are yellow, tubular, 5-lobed. **Stems:** Upright, usually leafless, hairy, up to 2½′ tall. **Leaves:** Basal, ovate, heart-shaped at base, without teeth; densely hairy, up to 15″ long and 6″ wide. **Season:** May–July. **Habitat:** Grasslands, open forests. **Range** (*see map*): Areas 4, 7–10, C. **Family:** Aster. **Comments:** This species is distinguished by its densely hairy, toothless basal leaves. Deltoid balsamroot, *B. deltoidea*, has only sparsely hairy leaves; lobed-leaf balsamroot, *B. hookeri*, has deeply lobed basal leaves.

▲ Prairie Dock
Ray and disk flowers.
Basal leaves only.

▲ Goldenweed
Ray and disk flowers.
Basal leaves only.

▼ Arrowleaf Balsamroot
Ray and disk flowers.
Basal leaves only.

▲ Woolly Flower
Ray and disk flowers.
Basal and alternate leaves.

YELLOW

ASTER FAMILY

Heartleaf Arnica, *Arnica cordifolia*

Flowers: Crowded into several heads up to 4″ across. Ray flowers number 10–15, yellow, pointed. Disk flowers are yellow, tubular, 5-lobed. **Stems:** Upright, hairy, unbranched, up to 20″ tall. **Leaves:** 2–4 opposite pairs, simple, ovate to lanceolate, heart-shaped at the base, with or without teeth; smooth or hairy. **Season:** April–Sept. **Habitat:** Woods. **Range** (*see map*): Areas 3, 4, 7–10, A–D. **Family:** Aster. **Comments:** Meadow arnica, *A. chamissonis*, has 5 or more pairs of leaves on the stem.

Tickseed, *Coreopsis lanceolata*

Flowers: Crowded together into several heads up to 3″ across. Ray flowers number 8, yellow, notched at tip, up to 1½″ long. Disk flowers are yellow, tubular, 5-lobed. **Stems:** Upright, smooth or hairy, up to 2′ tall. **Leaves:** Basal and opposite, narrowly lanceolate, without teeth; smooth or hairy, up to 4″ long. **Season:** May–July. **Habitat:** Fields and roadsides. **Range** (*see map*): Areas 1–3, 5, 6, C, E. **Family:** Aster. **Comments:** This species is distinguished from other tickseeds by its narrow, toothless leaves. Tickseeds with similar flower heads are the large-flowered tickseed, *C. grandiflora*, which has much divided leaves; and trefoil tickseed, *C. tripteris*, with slightly smaller flower heads and leaves divided into 3 leaflets.

Rosinweed, *Silphium integrifolium*

Flowers: Crowded together into several heads up to 2″ across. Ray flowers number 12–18, yellow, shallowly notched at tip. Disk flowers are yellow, tubular, 5-lobed. **Stems:** Upright, branched, smooth or hairy, up to 5′ tall. **Leaves:** Opposite, simple, narrowly ovate, with or without teeth; rough-hairy, up to 4″ long. **Season:** July–Aug. **Habitat:** Prairies. **Range** (*see map*): Areas 2, 3, 5, 6. **Family:** Aster. **Comments:** A similar species with similar flower heads is cup-plant, *S. perfoliatum*, whose opposite leaves meet on the stem to form cup-like structures that hold water.

Narrow-leaved Sunflower, *Helianthus angustifolius*

Flowers: Crowded together into a few heads up to 2½″ across. Ray flowers number 10–20, yellow, pointed at tip. Disk flowers are purple, tubular, 5-lobed. **Stems:** Upright, hairy, up to 2′ tall. **Leaves:** Opposite or alternate, simple, very narrow, without teeth; hairy, up to 10″ long, up to ½″ wide. **Season:** Aug–Oct. **Habitat:** Swamps, wet areas. **Range** (*see map*): Areas 1–3, 6. **Family:** Aster. **Comments:** This species is distinguished by its very narrow leaves, some of which are opposite and some alternate. Another sunflower with both alternate and opposite leaves is sawtooth sunflower, *H. grosseserratus*, which has a smooth stem that may reach 12′ tall.

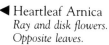
◀ Heartleaf Arnica
Ray and disk flowers.
Opposite leaves.

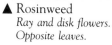

▲ Tickseed
Ray and disk flowers.
Opposite leaves.

▲ Rosinweed
Ray and disk flowers.
Opposite leaves.

▼ Narrow-leaved Sunflower
Ray and disk flowers. Opposite or alternate leaves.

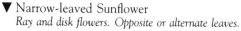

ASTER FAMILY

Goldeneye, *Viguiera multiflora*

Flowers: Crowded together into several heads up to 1½" across. Ray flowers number 12–20, yellow, up to ¾" long. Disk flowers are yellow, tubular. **Stems:** Upright, branched, smooth or hairy, up to 3' tall. **Leaves:** Upper are alternate, lower are opposite; simple, lanceolate, toothed or toothless; sparsely hairy, up to 3" long and 1" wide. **Season:** July–Sept. **Habitat:** Open, usually dry areas. **Range** (*see map*): Areas 7–10. **Family:** Aster. **Comments:** Narrow-leaved goldeneye, *V. longifolia*, has leaves up to ½" wide.

Swamp Marigold, *Bidens aristosa*

Flowers: Crowded together into many heads up to 2" across, with up to 10 green leaf-like structures (bracts) beneath each head. Ray flowers number 10–20, yellow, up to 1¼" long. Disk flowers are yellow, tubular. **Stems:** Upright, usually smooth, up to 4' tall. **Leaves:** Opposite, pinnately divided; somewhat hairy, up to 6" long. **Season:** Aug–Nov. **Habitat:** Wet ground. **Range** (*see map*): Areas 1–3, 6. **Family:** Aster. **Comments:** The fruits, often known as beggar-ticks, stick to clothing because of their barbed bristles. Very similar is the plains swamp marigold, *B. polylepis*, which has 12 or more green bracts beneath each flowering head.

Winged Crownbeard, *Verbesina alternifolia*

Flowers: Crowded into several heads up to 2¼" across. Ray flowers number up to 10, more or less hanging downward, up to 1½" long. Disk flowers are yellow, tubular, forming a spherical disk. **Stems:** Upright, hairy, usually with a narrow green wing. **Leaves:** Alternate, simple, lanceolate, usually toothed; rough-hairy, up to 10" long and 3" wide. **Season:** Aug–Oct. **Habitat:** Woods. **Range** (*see map*): Areas 1–3, 5, 6, E. **Family:** Aster. **Comments:** This species is readily recognized by its few ray flowers, which tend to hang downward. Western crownbeard, *V. encelioides*, has 10–15 ray flowers per head and leaves that are ovate.

Narrow-leaved Sneezeweed, *Helenium amarum*

Flowers: Crowded together into several heads up to 1½" across. Ray flowers number 5–10, yellow, 3-toothed at the tip, hanging downward, up to ½" long. Disk flowers are yellow, tubular, forming a round disk about ½" in diameter. **Stems:** Upright, branched, mostly smooth, up to 18" tall. **Leaves:** Almost needle-like, very numerous, up to 3" long. **Season:** June–Oct. **Habitat:** Woods, prairies, fields, roadsides. **Range** (*see map*): Areas 1–3, 5, 6, 10. **Family:** Aster. **Comments:** This sneezeweed is recognized by its abundant needle-like leaves. Autumn sneezeweed, *H. autumnale*, has winged stems and a yellow disk; winged sneezeweed, *H. flexuosum*, has winged stems and a brown disk.

▲ Goldeneye
Ray and disk flowers.
Some leaves opposite.

▲ Swamp Marigold
Ray and disk flowers.
Opposite leaves.

▲ Winged Crownbeard
Ray and disk flowers. Alternate leaves.

▲ Narrow-leaved Sneezeweed
Ray and disk flowers. Alternate leaves.

ASTER FAMILY

Orange Sneezeweed, *Dugaldia hoopesii*

Flowers: Crowded together into many heads up to 3″ across. Ray flowers are orange-yellow to yellow, very narrow, up to 1″ long, 3-toothed at tip, hanging downward. Disk flowers are yellow, tubular, forming a spherical disk up to 1″ across. **Stems:** Upright, hairy, bearing few leaves, up to 4′ tall. **Leaves:** Alternate and basal, simple, lanceolate, the lowermost up to 12″ long. **Season:** July–Sept. **Habitat:** Wet meadows. **Range** (*see map*): Areas 7–10. **Family:** Aster. **Comments:** This species contains substances that cause sheep poisoning.

Mule's Ears, *Wyethia amplexicaulis*

Flowers: Crowded together into heads up to 5″ across. Ray flowers number 13–21, yellow. Disk flowers are yellow, tubular, 5-lobed. **Stems:** Upright, smooth, in clumps, up to 2½′ tall. **Leaves:** Alternate, simple, lanceolate, with or without teeth; smooth, up to 16″ long, at least 1¾″ wide. **Season:** May–July. **Habitat:** Open woods, meadows. **Range** (*see map*): Areas 8, 9, C. **Family:** Aster. **Comments:** The crowded leaves on the stem distinguish this species from the similar arrowleaf balsamroot, *Balsamorhiza sagittata*. Rough mule's ears, *W. scabra*, has narrow leaves up to ¾″ wide.

Desert Marigold, *Baileya multiradiata*

Flowers: Crowded together into many heads up to 2″ across. Ray flowers are numerous, yellow, notched at tip. Disk flowers are yellow, tubular. **Stems:** Upright, with gray woolly hairs, up to 20″ tall. **Leaves:** Alternate, pinnately divided; with gray woolly hairs, up to 3″ long. **Season:** May–July. **Habitat:** Open areas and open woods. **Range** (*see map*): Areas 6–8, 10. **Family:** Aster. **Comments:** This gorgeous species often occurs in large, dense patches. Other desert marigolds are *B. pleniradiata*, with heads up to 1″ across; and *B. pauciradiata*, with only 5–8 rays per head.

Golden Yarrow, *Eriophyllum lanatum*

Flowers: Crowded together in several heads up to 2½″ across. Ray flowers number 8–12, yellow, up to ¾″ long. Disk flowers are yellow, tubular. **Stems:** Upright, with white woolly hairs, up to 2′ tall. **Leaves:** Alternate, simple, narrow, toothed or lobed; with white woolly hairs, up to 3″ long. **Season:** May–July. **Habitat:** Dry, usually open areas. **Range** (*see map*): Areas 8–10, C. **Family:** Aster. **Comments:** The distinguishing features of this showy wildflower are the white-woolly leaves and stems.

Orange Sneezeweed ▶
Ray and disk flowers.
Alternate leaves.

▲ Mule's Ears
Ray and disk flowers.
Alternate leaves.

▲ Desert Marigold
Ray and disk flowers.
Alternate leaves.

▼ Golden Yarrow
Ray and disk flowers. Alternate leaves.

YELLOW

ASTER FAMILY

Common Gumweed, *Grindelia squarrosa*

Flowers: Crowded together into several heads up to 2″ across. Ray flowers number 20–35 (but are sometimes absent), yellow, up to ⅔″ long. Disk flowers are yellow, tubular. **Stems:** Upright, branched, up to 3′ tall. **Leaves:** Alternate, simple, oblong to ovate, usually toothed; sticky, up to 3″ long and 1″ wide. **Season:** July–Oct. **Habitat:** Open areas. **Range** (*see map*): All areas except A. **Family:** Aster. **Comments:** Most gumweeds may be recognized by their sticky leaves. Similar to the common gumweed is the lance-leaved gumweed, *G. lanceolata*, which has narrower leaves with bristle-tipped teeth.

Common Sunflower, *Helianthus annuus*

Flowers: Many, crowded into huge heads up to 10″ across. Ray flowers are numerous, yellow. Disk flowers are numerous, brown, tubular. **Stems:** Upright, branched, hairy, up to 10′ tall. **Leaves:** Alternate, simple, ovate, heart-shaped at base; with rough hairs, up to 12″ long. **Season:** Aug–Sept. **Habitat:** Open areas. **Range** (*see map*): All areas except B. **Family:** Aster. **Comments:** The seeds of this large, familiar sunflower are eaten by humans, birds, squirrels, and other animals. Similar is the stalked sunflower, *H. petiolaris*, but this species does not have leaves heart-shaped at the base.

Golden Aster, *Heterotheca villosa*

Flowers: Crowded together into several heads up to 1¼″ across. Ray flowers number 15–35, yellow, more than ¼″ long. Disk flowers are yellow, tubular. **Stems:** Upright, clustered, hairy, up to 3′ tall. **Leaves:** Alternate, simple, oblong to elliptic, usually without teeth; hairy, up to 2¾″ long. **Season:** July–Oct. **Habitat:** Dry, open areas. **Range** (*see map*): Areas 2–10, C, D. **Family:** Aster. **Comments:** The leaves of this wildflower are sometimes silvery-silky. Camphor weed, *H. subaxillaris*, is similar, but the ray flowers are less than ¼″ long.

Snakeweed, *Gutierrezia sarothrae*

Flowers: Crowded together into very numerous small heads. Ray flowers number 3–7, yellow, less than ¼″ long. Disk flowers number 2–6, yellow, tubular. **Stems:** Upright, much branched, up to 3′ tall. **Leaves:** Alternate, simple, very narrow, without teeth; not hairy, up to 2½″ long and ⅛″ wide. **Season:** Aug–Oct. **Habitat:** Open areas. **Range** (*see map*): Areas 4–10, C, D. **Family:** Aster. **Comments:** This is a very common plant of prairies and plains. The similar small-headed snakeweed, *G. microcephala*, has only 2 or 3 ray flowers per head.

▲ Common Gumweed
Ray and disk flowers. Alternate leaves.

▼ Common Sunflower
Ray and disk flowers.
Alternate leaves.

▼ Golden Aster
Ray and disk flowers.
Mostly alternate leaves.

▼ Snakeweed
Ray and disk flowers. Alternate leaves.

ASTER FAMILY

Yellow Coneflower, *Ratibida columnifera*

Flowers: Crowded together into heads up to 1½″ long and ¾″ across. Ray flowers number 3–7, yellow, often with purple markings, up to 1¼″ long. Disk flowers are dark purple, tubular, forming a columnar disk up to 1½″ long. **Stems:** Upright, branched, hairy, up to 3½′ tall. **Leaves:** Alternate, pinnately divided, hairy. **Season:** June–Aug. **Habitat:** Prairies, open areas. **Range** (*see map*): Areas 1–9, C–E. **Family:** Aster. **Comments:** The long, columnar disk readily distinguishes this prairie wildflower. Drooping coneflower, *R. pinnata*, has a disk only ½″–¾″ long and drooping, pale yellow rays up to 3″ long.

Black-eyed Susan, *Rudbeckia hirta*

Flowers: Crowded together into showy heads up to 4″ across. Ray flowers number 12–20, yellow, notched at tip. Disk flowers are purple-brown, tubular, 5-lobed, forming a low conical disk. **Stems:** Upright, usually branched, hairy, up to 3½′ tall. **Leaves:** Alternate, simple, lanceolate, sparsely toothed; hairy, up to 2″ across. **Season:** June–Oct. **Habitat:** Fields, prairies, open areas. **Range** (*see map*): Areas 1–9, C–F. **Family:** Aster. **Comments:** Other species with yellow rays and purple-brown disks include the lobed-leaf black-eyed susan, *R. triloba*, with lobed leaves and 6–12 ray flowers per head; and woolly black-eyed susan, *R. subtomentosa*, with lobed leaves and 12–20 ray flowers per head.

Tall Goldenrod, *Solidago canadensis*

Flowers: Crowded into many small heads about ¼″ high. Ray flowers number 7–17, yellow, about ⅛″ long. Disk flowers are yellow, tubular, 5-lobed. **Stems:** Upright, branched, smooth or hairy, up to 8′ tall. **Leaves:** Alternate, simple, lanceolate, usually toothed; hairy, up to 1″ across. **Season:** Aug–Oct. **Habitat:** Fields, woods, open areas. **Range** (*see map*): Areas 1–9, C–F. **Family:** Aster. **Comments:** There are about 100 different species of goldenrod in the world, most of them native in North America. Another common goldenrod is the gray goldenrod, *S. nemoralis*, which is usually less than 3′ tall and which has densely short-hairy stems and leaves.

Stiff Goldenrod, *Solidago rigida*

Flowers: Crowded into heads about ½″ across, the heads arranged in a rounded cluster. Ray flowers number 8–14, yellow. Disk flowers are yellow, tubular. **Stems:** Upright, smooth or hairy, up to 4½′ tall. **Leaves:** Basal leaves are elliptic to ovate, hairy, up to 9″ long; stem leaves are alternate, broadly elliptic, hairy, up to 2″ long. **Season:** July–Oct. **Habitat:** Prairies, open areas. **Range** (*see map*): Areas 1–6, C–E. **Family:** Aster. **Comments:** This goldenrod is distinguished by its numerous heads arranged in a round-topped cluster.

▲ Yellow Coneflower
Ray and disk flowers.
Alternate leaves.

▲ Black-eyed Susan
Ray and disk flowers.
Alternate leaves.

▲ Tall Goldenrod
Ray and disk flowers.
Alternate leaves.

◄ Stiff Goldenrod
Ray and disk flowers.
Alternate leaves.

ASTER FAMILY

Small's Groundsel, *Senecio anonymus*

Flowers: Crowded into numerous heads up to ¾" across. Ray flowers number 8–15, yellow, up to ⅜" long. Disk flowers are yellow, tubular. **Stems:** Upright, densely woolly at the base, up to 2½' tall. **Leaves:** Basal leaves are simple, elliptic, toothed, hairy, up to 12" long; stem leaves are alternate, deeply cleft, much smaller. **Season:** May–June. **Habitat:** Open woods, meadows. **Range** (*see map*): Areas 1, 2. **Family:** Aster. **Comments:** The very long, elliptic basal leaves and deeply divided stem leaves distinguish Small's groundsel. Prairie groundsel, *S. pauperculus*, is similar but has much shorter basal leaves and stems smooth at the base.

Pale Agoseris, *Agoseris glauca*

Flowers: Crowded into solitary heads at the top of leafless stalks, each head up to 1¼" across. Ray flowers are numerous, pale yellow, blunt, with several notches at the tip. No disk flowers. **Stems:** Leafless, smooth, to 2' tall, with milky sap. **Leaves:** All basal, lanceolate, without teeth but sometimes lobed; smooth, up to 14" long, with milky sap. **Season:** May–Sept. **Habitat:** Prairies, plains, open woods. **Range** (*see map*): Areas 3–5, 7–9, A–E. **Family:** Aster. **Comments:** Orange agoseris, *A. aurantiaca*, has orange flower heads. Common dandelion, *Taraxacum officinale*, usually has leaves more deeply lobed.

Desert Dandelion, *Malacothrix glabrata*

Flowers: Crowded into dense heads up to 1½" across. Ray flowers are numerous, yellow, up to ¾" long. No disk flowers. **Stems:** Upright, smooth, without leaves, up to 14" tall, with milky sap. **Leaves:** All basal, deeply cleft, smooth, up to 5" long, with milky sap. **Season:** March–June. **Habitat:** Deserts. **Range** (*see map*): Areas 7–10. **Family:** Aster. **Comments:** Another desert dandelion, *M. sonchoides*, has a few leaves on the stem.

False Dandelion, *Pyrrhopappus carolinianus*

Flowers: Crowded together into solitary heads up to 1½" across. Ray flowers are numerous, pale yellow, blunt, with several notches at the tip. No disk flowers. **Stems:** Upright, branched, usually smooth, up to 3½' tall, with milky sap. **Leaves:** Basal and alternate, simple, oblong to lanceolate, with or without teeth or lobes; smooth, with milky sap. **Season:** May–June. **Habitat:** Prairies, fields. **Range** (*see map*): Areas 1–3, 5, 6. **Family:** Aster. **Comments:** The tall, smooth, somewhat leafy stems distinguish this false dandelion. Large-flowered false dandelion, *P. grandiflorus*, usually has leafless stems.

▲ Small's Groundsel
Ray and disk flowers.
Alternate leaves.

Pale Agoseris ▶
Ray flowers only. Milky sap.

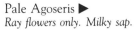

▲ Desert Dandelion
Ray flowers only. Milky sap.

False Dandelion ▶
Ray flowers only. Milky sap.

ASTER FAMILY

Sow Thistle, *Sonchus oleraceus*

Flowers: Crowded into several heads in a cluster, each head up to 1¼" across. Ray flowers are numerous, yellow. No disk flowers. **Stems:** Upright, smooth, up to 10' tall, with milky sap. **Leaves:** Lower leaves deeply lobed; upper leaves sharply toothed with spiny teeth, smooth. **Season:** July–Oct. **Habitat:** Fields, open areas. **Range** (*see map*): All areas. **Family:** Aster. **Comments:** Prickly sow thistle, *S. asper*, has leaves much more prickly; field sow thistle, *S. arvensis*, has heads at least 1½" across.

Goat's-beard, *Tragopogon dubius*

Flowers: Crowded together into solitary heads up to 3" across, with green leaf-like structures (bracts) that are longer than the rays. Ray flowers are numerous, yellow, up to 1½" long. No disk flowers. **Stems:** Upright, smooth, up to 2' tall, with milky sap. **Leaves:** Alternate, simple, long-tapering at the tip, without teeth; smooth, up to ¾" across, with milky sap. **Season:** May–July. **Habitat:** Fields, open areas. **Range** (*see map*): Areas 1–10, B–E. **Family:** Aster. **Comments:** Another similar yellow-flowered goat's-beard is *T. pratensis*, but its ray flowers are longer than the green bracts. Purple goat's-beard, *T. porrifolius*, has purple ray flowers.

RADIAL SYMMETRY

Yellow Pitcher Plant, *Sarracenia flava*

Flowers: Solitary at the tip of a leafless stalk, nodding, up to 4" across. **Petals:** 5, bright yellow. **Stems:** Leafless, up to 2' tall. **Leaves:** Basal, hollow and pitcher-shaped, with a terminal lid, each leaf up to 2' long. **Season:** May. **Habitat:** Bogs. **Range** (*see map*): Areas 1, 2. **Family:** Pitcher Plant. **Comments:** The leaves of this plant trap insects, from which the plant obtains nutrients. Purple pitcher plant, *S. purpurea*, has purple flowers and leaves only up to 8" long.

Yellow Columbine, *Aquilegia chrysantha*

Flowers: Few, on slender stalks, but not nodding, up to 3" across. **Petals:** 5, yellow, prolonged backward into spurs up to 3" long. **Stems:** Upright, much branched, usually hairy, up to 4' tall. **Leaves:** Basal and alternate, divided into several leaflets. **Season:** July–Aug. **Habitat:** Moist, shaded areas. **Range** (*see map*): Areas 6–8. **Family:** Buttercup. **Comments:** Long-spur columbine, *A. longissima*, another yellow-flowered species, has spurs up to 6" long.

▲ Sow Thistle
Ray flowers only. Milky sap.

▲ Goat's-beard
Ray flowers only. Milky sap.

▲ Yellow Pitcher Plant
5 separated petals. Pitcher leaves.

Yellow Columbine ▶
5 separated spur-like petals.

RADIAL SYMMETRY

Wild Parsnip, *Pastinaca sativa*

Flowers: Many, borne in large clusters (umbels), each flower about ⅙″ across. **Petals:** 5, separated. **Stems:** Upright, branched, smooth or hairy, up to 5′ tall. **Leaves:** Alternate, pinnately compound; the leaflets are oval to ovate, toothed, smooth or hairy, up to 3″ long. **Season:** May–Oct. **Habitat:** Open areas. **Range** (*see map*): All areas. **Family:** Carrot. **Comments:** The roots of this robust species may be eaten as vegetables. Another robust, yellow-flowered member of the carrot family is sweet fennel, *Foeniculum vulgare*, but its leaf segments are extremely narrow.

Stiff Flax, *Linum rigidum*

Flowers: Formed in the axils of the leaves, up to 1½″ across. **Petals:** 5, separated, about ¾″ long. **Stems:** Upright, branched, smooth, up to 1½′ tall. **Leaves:** Alternate, simple, very narrow, without teeth; smooth, up to 1″ long. **Season:** May–June. **Habitat:** Prairies, plains. **Range** (*see map*): Areas 3–9, C, D. **Family:** Flax. **Comments:** There are several similar yellow-flowered flaxes, including woodland flax, *L. medium*, which has petals less than ½″ long.

Klamath Weed, *Hypericum perforatum*

Flowers: Many, in terminal clusters, each flower up to 1″ across. **Petals:** 5, separated, black-spotted only along the edges. **Stems:** Upright, branched, smooth, up to 2½′ tall. **Leaves:** Opposite, simple, oblong, without teeth; smooth, black-dotted, up to 1″ long. **Season:** June–Sept. **Habitat:** Fields, open areas. **Range** (*see map*): Areas 1–6, 8–10, C, E, F. **Family:** St. John's-wort. **Comments:** A California species with similar flowers is gold wire, *H. concinnum*, but its stems are wiry and only up to 16″ tall.

Scouler's St. John's-wort, *Hypericum formosum*

Flowers: Several, in terminal clusters, up to ¾″ across. **Petals:** 5, separated, black-spotted. **Stems:** Upright, slender, smooth, up to 3′ tall. **Leaves:** Opposite, simple, oval to oblong, without teeth; smooth, up to 2″ long, black-spotted along the edges. **Season:** June–Sept. **Habitat:** Hills and mountains. **Range** (*see map*): Areas 7–10, C. **Family:** St. John's-wort. **Comments:** Another common species with black-spotted petals is spotted St. John's-wort, *H. punctatum*, but its leaves are dotted across the entire surface.

▲ Wild Parsnip
5 separated petals. 5 stamens.

▲ Stiff Flax
5 separated petals.
5 stamens.

▲ Klamath Weed
5 separated petals. Many stamens.

▲ Scouler's
St. John's-wort
5 separated petals.
Many stamens.

RADIAL SYMMETRY

Yellow Saxifrage, *Saxifraga flagellaris*

Flowers: Solitary or a few per stem, up to ¼" across. **Petals:** 5, separated.
Stems: Upright, hairy, up to 6" tall. **Leaves:** Basal leaves crowded,
oblong, without teeth, spine-tipped; stem leaves alternate, oblong. **Season:**
July–Aug. **Habitat:** Rocky areas in high mountains. **Range** (*see map*):
Areas 7–9, A, C. **Family:** Saxifrage. **Comments:** Other alpine Rocky
Mountain saxifrages include purple saxifrage, *S. oppositifolia*, with purple
flowers; brook saxifrage, *S. arguta*, with white petals tinged with yellow;
spotted saxifrage, *S. bronchialis*, with white petals dotted with purple; and
diamondleaf saxifrage, *S. rhomboidea*, with white petals.

Yellow Wood Sorrel, *Oxalis stricta*

Flowers: Several, in terminal clusters, each flower up to ½" long. **Petals:**
5, separated, sometimes with a reddish center. **Stems:** Upright, branched,
smooth or sparsely hairy, up to 10" tall. **Leaves:** Alternate, divided into
3 leaflets, each leaflet broadest at the notched tip, smooth or nearly hairy.
Season: April–Sept. **Habitat:** Woods, fields, open areas. **Range** (*see
map*): Areas 1–9, C–F. **Family:** Wood Sorrel. **Comments:** This species
contains oxalic acid, which gives it a sour taste. Very similar is hairy wood
sorrel, *O. dillenii*, which often has dense white hairs on the stem.

Velvetleaf, *Abutilon theophrastii*

Flowers: Few, arising from the leaf axils, up to ¼" across. **Petals:** 5,
separated, broad and blunt at the tip. **Stems:** Upright, branched, with
velvet hairs up to 6' tall. **Leaves:** Alternate, simple, broadly ovate, heart-
shaped at the base, mostly without teeth; with velvet hairs, up to 10"
long. **Season:** Aug–Oct. **Habitat:** Open areas. **Range** (*see map*): Areas
1–8, 10, D–F. **Family:** Mallow. **Comments:** This species can become an
aggressive weed in agricultural fields. Wright's velvetleaf, *A. wrightii*, is a
similar, smaller species with sticky hairs.

Blazing Star, *Mentzelia laevicaulis*

Flowers: Few, but large and star-shaped, up to 5" across. **Petals:** 5,
separated, lemon-yellow, pointed. **Stems:** Upright, robust, white, up to
3' tall. **Leaves:** Alternate, simple, lanceolate, coarsely toothed; rough to
the touch, up to 12" long. **Season:** June–Sept. **Habitat:** Dry, open areas.
Range (*see map*): Areas 4, 8–10, C. **Family:** Stick-leaf. **Comments:**
Similar is white-bracted stick-leaf, *M. involucrata*, with much smaller, very
pale yellow petals; and yellow stick-leaf, *M. multiflora*, with yellow flowers
up to 4" across and narrowly lanceolate leaves.

▲ Yellow Wood Sorrel
  5 separated petals.
  10 stamens.

▲ Yellow Saxifrage
  5 separated petals. 10 stamens.

▼ Blazing Star
  5 separated petals. Many stamens.

▲ Velvetleaf
  5 separated petals.
  Many stamens.

RADIAL SYMMETRY

Marsh Marigold, *Caltha palustris*

Flowers: Few, terminal or arising from the leaf axils, up to 1½" across. **Petals:** None, but the 5 sepals are petal-like, separated, yellow. **Stems:** Usually upright, hollow, smooth, branched above, to 2' tall. **Leaves:** Basal and alternate, simple, heart-shaped, toothed; smooth. **Season:** April–May. **Habitat:** Bogs, swamps, moist meadows, wet woods. **Range** (*see map*): All areas except 6–8. **Family:** Buttercup. **Comments:** This is one of the most attractive wetland wildflowers. White marsh marigold, *C. leptosepala*, has white flowers, sometimes bluish tinged on the outside.

Tall Buttercup, *Ranunculus acris*

Flowers: Several, arising from the upper leaf axils, each flower up to 1" across. **Petals:** 5, separated, yellow, rounded at the tip. **Stems:** Upright, branched, hairy, up to 3' tall. **Leaves:** Basal leaves are divided into 3–7 smooth, toothed leaflets; stem leaves are alternate, 3-lobed or unlobed, smooth. **Season:** May–Aug. **Habitat:** Moist, open areas. **Range** (*see map*): Areas 1–5, 8–10, A, C–F. **Family:** Buttercup. **Comments:** Bulbous buttercup, *R. bulbosus*, has similar flowers but usually is only about 1½' tall and has a swollen, bulbous base.

Hispid Buttercup, *Ranunculus hispidus*

Flowers: Few, in terminal clusters, each flower up to 1¼" across. **Petals:** 5, separated, at least ½" long. **Stems:** Upright, branched, densely hairy, up to 20" tall. **Leaves:** Basal and alternate, divided into 3- or 5-lobed or sharply toothed leaflets; densely hairy. **Season:** March–May. **Habitat:** Dry woods. **Range** (*see map*): Areas 1–6, E. **Family:** Buttercup. **Comments:** Fasciculate buttercup, *R. fascicularis*, is very similar but has clusters of thickened roots.

Indian Strawberry, *Duchesnea indica*

Flowers: Solitary, arising opposite the leaves, each flower up to ¾" across. **Petals:** 5, separated, blunt at the tip. **Stems:** Mostly creeping along ground, hairy. **Leaves:** Basal and alternate, divided into 3 leaflets; the leaflets are ovate to elliptic, toothed, hairy. **Season:** April–Aug. **Habitat:** Open areas. **Range** (*see map*): Areas 1–3, 6, 9, 10, C. **Family:** Rose. **Comments:** Although the ripe, red fruits resemble miniature strawberries, the berries are not sweet and are scarcely edible.

▲ Marsh Marigold
5 separated petal-like parts. Many stamens.

▲ Tall Buttercup
5 separated petals. Many stamens.

▲ Hispid Buttercup
5 separated petals. Many stamens.

▲ Indian Strawberry
5 separated petals. Many stamens.

RADIAL SYMMETRY

Sticky Cinquefoil, *Potentilla glandulosa*

Flowers: Several, in terminal clusters, each flower up to ¾" across. **Petals:** 5, separated. **Stems:** Upright, clumped, hairy, up to 1½' tall. **Leaves:** Basal leaves divided into 7 or 9 leaflets; stem leaves divided into 3 or 5 leaflets. **Season:** May–July. **Habitat:** Open areas. **Range** (*see map*): Areas 2, 4, 7–10, B, C. **Family:** Rose. **Comments:** "Cinquefoil" refers to 5 leaflets that many of these species possess. Common silverweed, *P. anserina*, is similar but has a creeping stem with solitary flowers.

Sulphur Cinquefoil, *Potentilla recta*

Flowers: Several, in terminal clusters, each flower up to ¾" across. **Petals:** 5, separated, notched at tip. **Stems:** Upright, branched, hairy, up to 2' tall. **Leaves:** Alternate, divided into 5–7 coarsely toothed, hairy leaflets. **Season:** May–July. **Habitat:** Open areas. **Range** (*see map*): Areas 1–6, 8–10, C–F. **Family:** Rose. **Comments:** Norwegian cinquefoil, *P. norvegica*, has flowers less than ½" across and leaves divided into 3 leaflets.

Spatterdock, *Nuphar luteum*

Flowers: Solitary, borne usually just above the surface of the water, up to 1¾" across. **Petals:** Numerous, separated, shorter than the 5 or 6 petal-like sepals. **Stems:** Underwater. **Leaves:** Ovate, heart-shaped at base, without teeth; shiny, smooth, up to 15" long. **Season:** June–Aug. **Habitat:** Lakes, ponds. **Range** (*see map*): All areas. **Family:** Water Lily. **Comments:** This aquatic species is extremely variable in appearance. Sometimes the petals have a reddish tinge.

Water Lotus, *Nelumbo lutea*

Flowers: Solitary, elevated on stout stalks above the water, each flower up to 10" across. **Petals:** Numerous, separated. **Stems:** Underwater, except for the stalk bearing the flower. **Leaves:** Round, lying flat on the water, up to 2½' across, attached at their center to the leaf stalk. **Season:** June–Aug. **Habitat:** Lakes, ponds, quiet rivers. **Range** (*see map*): Areas 1–3, 5, 6, E. **Family:** Water Lotus. **Comments:** The fruits are hard, woody, and flat; they contain spherical seeds nearly ½" in diameter.

▲ Sticky Cinquefoil
5 separated petals. Many stamens.

Sulphur Cinquefoil ▶
5 separated petals. Many stamens.

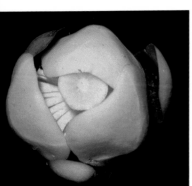

◀ Spatterdock
Many separated petals.
Many stamens. Aquatic.

▼ Water Lotus
Many separated petals.
Many stamens. Aquatic.

RADIAL SYMMETRY

Cliff Prickly Pear, *Opuntia phaeacantha*

Flowers: Solitary, up to 3″ across. **Petals:** Numerous, often reddish at the base, separated. **Stems:** Blue-green, with flattened spines, the succulent joints often in chains. **Leaves:** None. **Season:** April–May. **Habitat:** Dry areas. **Range** (*see map*): Areas 3–8, 10. **Family:** Cactus. **Comments:** Sometimes the succulent joints become reddish purple.

Common Prickly Pear, *Opuntia compressa*

Flowers: Solitary, up to 3″ across. **Petals:** Numerous, separated. **Stems:** Succulent, flattened, oblong to circular, up to 4½″ long. **Leaves:** None. **Season:** March–July. **Habitat:** Dry, open areas. **Range** (*see map*): Areas 3–10, C–E. **Family:** Cactus. **Comments:** This is the most common of the prickly pears that have flat pads and yellow flowers.

Large Buttercup, *Ranunculus macranthus*

Flowers: Showy, up to 2″ across. **Petals:** 8–18, separated. **Stems:** More or less upright, hollow, hairy, usually up to 18″ tall. **Leaves:** Basal and alternate, usually divided into 3–7 smooth or hairy leaflets. **Season:** March–June. **Habitat:** Wet soil. **Range** (*see map*): Areas 6, 7. **Family:** Buttercup. **Comments:** This species has the largest flowers of any buttercup in North America. Swamp buttercup, *R. septentrionalis*, also a species of wet habitats, has flowers up to 1½″ across and only 5 petals.

Small Prickly Pear, *Opuntia fragilis*

Flowers: Solitary, up to 1¾″ across. **Petals:** Numerous, separated. **Stems:** Succulent, lying flat, some of the joints nearly spherical, each joint less than 2″ long. **Leaves:** None. **Season:** June–July. **Habitat:** Dry soil in prairies and plains. **Range** (*see map*): Areas 3–10, C–E. **Family:** Cactus. **Comments:** *Opuntia* is a huge group of cacti that shows great diversity. Some species have flattened stems, or "pads," others have cylindrical stems; some have pink or rose flowers, others have yellow.

▲ Cliff Prickly Pear
Many separated petals.
Many stamens.

▼ Common Prickly Pear
Many separated petals.
Many stamens.

Small Prickly Pear ▶
Many separated petals.
Many stamens.

▼ Large Buttercup
Many separated petals.
Many stamens.

RADIAL SYMMETRY

Yellow Rocket, *Barbarea vulgaris*

Flowers: Many, both terminal and arising from the leaf axils, each flower up to ⅓" across. **Petals:** 4, separated. **Stems:** Upright, branched, smooth, up to 2' tall. **Leaves:** Basal leaves divided into 3–9 smooth segments, the terminal segment the largest; stem leaves alternate, simple, toothed, smooth. **Season:** April–June. **Habitat:** Open areas. **Range** (*see map*): Areas 1–6, 8–10, B–F. **Family:** Mustard. **Comments:** Northern rocket, *B. orthoceras*, has flowers only ¼" across; early rocket, *B. verna*, has 9–19 basal leaf segments.

Field Mustard, *Brassica campestris*

Flowers: Several, both terminal and arising from the leaf axils, each flower up to ½" across. **Petals:** 4, separated. **Stems:** Upright, branched, usually smooth, up to 2½' tall. **Leaves:** Basal leaves divided into several smooth lobes; stem leaves alternate, toothed, smooth. **Season:** May–Oct. **Habitat:** Open areas. **Range** (*see map*): All areas except A. **Family:** Mustard. **Comments:** Black mustard, *B. nigra*, has similar flowers but bristly-hairy stems; brown mustard, *B. juncea*, has larger flowers ½" or more across and smooth stems.

Desert Plume, *Stanleya pinnata*

Flowers: Many, in long spire-like clusters, each flower up to ⅝" long. **Petals:** 4, separated. **Stems:** Upright, robust, smooth, blue-green, up to 5' tall. **Leaves:** Basal leaves divided into several smooth segments; stem leaves alternate, smaller, smooth, usually divided into several segments. **Season:** May–July. **Habitat:** Dry soil, often in deserts. **Range** (*see map*): Areas 4–10. **Family:** Mustard. **Comments:** The wand-like clusters of flowers readily distinguish this species. White desert plume, *S. albescens*, has white flowers; lemon-flowered desert plume, *S. viridiflora*, has lemon-yellow to nearly white flowers.

Celandine Poppy, *Stylophorum diphyllum*

Flowers: 1–4 in clusters at the tip of the stem, up to 2" across. **Petals:** 4, separated, rounded at the tip. **Stems:** More or less upright, hairy, up to 12" tall, with yellow sap. **Leaves:** Basal and opposite, deeply lobed, hairy, up to 10" long, with yellow sap. **Season:** April–May. **Habitat:** Rich, moist woods. **Range** (*see map*): Areas 1–3, E. **Family:** Poppy. **Comments:** This gorgeous wildflower is distinguished by its 4 large petals and hairy, divided leaves. True celandine, *Chelidonium majus*, has smaller yellow flowers.

▲ Yellow Rocket
  4 separated petals. 6 stamens.

Field Mustard ▶
  4 separated petals. 6 stamens.

▼ Desert Plume
  4 separated petals. 6 stamens.

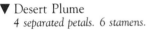

▼ Celandine Poppy
  4 separated petals. Many stamens.

RADIAL SYMMETRY

Common Evening Primrose, *Oenothera biennis*

Flowers: Up to 2½" across, opening in the evening. **Petals:** 4, separated, shallowly notched at the tip. **Stems:** Upright, branched or unbranched, hairy, up to 6' tall. **Leaves:** Alternate, simple, lanceolate, toothed; hairy, up to 6" long. **Season:** June–Oct. **Habitat:** Open areas. **Range** (*see map*): Areas 1–8, C–F. **Family:** Evening Primrose. **Comments:** The distinguishing field marks of this species are the tall hairy stems and large yellow flowers. Small-flowered evening primrose, *O. parviflora*, is similar but has flowers only about half as large; cleft evening primrose, *O. laciniata*, has cleft leaves.

Common Sundrops, *Oenothera fruticosa*

Flowers: Several, crowded in the leaf axils, each flower up to 2" across. **Petals:** 4, separated, showy. **Stems:** Upright, branched or unbranched, smooth or with some hairs, up to 24" tall. **Leaves:** Alternate, simple, very narrow to ovate, without teeth; sometimes hairy, up to 4" long. **Season:** May–Aug. **Habitat:** Dry woods, fields. **Range** (*see map*): Areas 1–3, 6, D–F. **Family:** Evening Primrose. **Comments:** Thread-leaved sundrops, *O. linifolia*, has smaller flowers and thread-like leaves.

Prairie Sundrops, *Oenothera pilosella*

Flowers: Up to 2" across, opening during the day. **Petals:** 4, separated. **Stems:** Upright, branched, smooth or hairy, up to 3' tall. **Leaves:** Alternate, simple, lanceolate, shallowly toothed; usually hairy, up to 4" long. **Season:** May–July. **Habitat:** Prairies and fields. **Range** (*see map*): Areas 1–3, E. **Family:** Evening Primrose. **Comments:** This species is distinguished by its erect flowers. Nodding sundrops, *O. perennis*, is very similar but has nodding flowers.

Yellow Star-grass, *Hypoxis hirsuta*

Flowers: 3 or more in a cluster, up to ¾" across, on hairy stalks. **Petal-like Parts:** 6, separated, oblong to lanceolate. **Stems:** Leafless, up to 8" tall. **Leaves:** All basal, long and narrow; conspicuously hairy, up to ¼" across. **Season:** April–May. **Habitat:** Dry, rocky woods; prairies. **Range** (*see map*): Areas 1–6, D, E. **Family:** Lily. **Comments:** *Hypoxis* is a bright little group of plants common in the southeastern U.S.A. Other species include smooth star-grass, *H. leptocarpa*, with nearly smooth leaves; narrow-leaved star-grass, *H. juncea*, with leaves about ⅟₁₆" across; and few-flowered star-grass, *H. micrantha*, with only 1 or 2 flowers per stem.

▲ Common Evening Primrose
  4 separated petals. 8 stamens.

▲ Common Sundrops
  4 separated petals. 8 stamens.

▲ Prairie Sundrops
  4 separated petals.
  8 stamens.

▲ Yellow Star-grass
  6 separated petal-like parts.
  3 stamens.

RADIAL SYMMETRY

Yellow Trout Lily, *Erythronium americanum*

Flowers: Solitary, nodding, up to 2″ long. **Petal-like Parts:** 6, separated, oblong, often speckled with maroon. **Stems:** Leafless, bearing only the single flower, up to 8″ long. **Leaves:** 1 or 2, basal, oblong-lanceolate, toothless; smooth, blotched with purple, up to 8″ long and 2″ wide. **Season:** March–May. **Habitat:** Rich woods. **Range** (*see map*): Areas 1– 3, 6, E, F. **Family:** Lily. **Comments:** Very similar, except for its white petal-like parts, is the white trout lily, *E. albidum*. Both species are sometimes called dog-tooth violets or adder's-tongues.

Yellow Bell, *Fritillaria pudica*

Flowers: Solitary, nodding, bell-shaped, up to 1″ long. **Petal-like Parts:** 6, separated. **Stems:** Upright, slender, smooth, up to 12″ tall. **Leaves:** Alternate, simple, toothless; smooth, up to 8″ long. **Season:** March–June. **Habitat:** Grasslands and open woods. **Range** (*see map*): Areas 4, 8–10, C. **Family:** Lily. **Comments:** The flowers often become reddish as they mature. This species is sometimes called yellow fritillary. Purple fritillary, *F. atropurpurea*, is a widespread species with brown-purple flowers.

Western Fawn Lily, *Erythronium grandiflorum*

Flowers: 1–5, nodding, up to 2″ long. **Petal-like Parts:** 6, separated, curving backward. **Stems:** Leafless, bearing only the flowers, up to 12″ long. **Leaves:** 1 or 2, basal, lanceolate, up to 8″ long and 2″ wide. **Season:** March–Aug. **Habitat:** Open areas, including open woods. **Range** (*see map*): Areas 7–10, C. **Family:** Lily. **Comments:** Glacier lily, *E. montanum*, an alpine species, has nodding white flowers.

Yellow Bellwort, *Uvularia grandiflora*

Flowers: Up to 1½″ long, drooping, on a curved, smooth stalk. **Petal-like Parts:** 6, separated, lanceolate. **Stems:** Upright, often branched, smooth, up to 1½′ tall. **Leaves:** Alternate, simple, oblong to oval, without teeth; smooth except for hairs on the veins, up to 4″ long, seemingly pierced near the base by the stem. **Season:** April–May. **Habitat:** Rich woods. **Range** (*see map*): Areas 1–6, E. **Family:** Lily. **Comments:** Perfoliate bellwort, *U. perfoliata*, is very similar but lacks hairs on the leaf veins; pale bellwort, *U. sessilifolia*, has straw-colored flowers less than 1″ long.

▲ Yellow Trout Lily
  6 separated petal-like parts.
  6 stamens.

▲ Yellow Bell
  6 separate petal-like parts.
  6 stamens.

▲ Western Fawn Lily
  6 separated petal-like parts.
  6 stamens.

▼ Yellow Bellwort
  6 separated petal-like parts. 6 stamens.

RADIAL SYMMETRY

Yellow Umbrella-plant, *Eriogonum flavum*

Flowers: Numerous, arranged in clusters (umbels), each flower up to ¼" long. **Petal-like Parts:** 6, separated, hairy on the outside. **Stems:** Upright, hairy, up to 8" tall. **Leaves:** Basal, simple, oblong; hairy, up to 1¾" long. **Season:** Aug–Sept. **Habitat:** Open areas. **Range** (*see map*): Areas 4, 5, 9, A, C, D. **Family:** Smartweed. **Comments:** More than 225 species of *Eriogonum* occur in North America, almost all of them in the West. Another common yellow-flowered species is desert trumpet, *E. inflatum*, which has conspicuous inflated areas on the stem.

Fiddle Head, *Amsinckia intermedia*

Flowers: Several, in elongated, semi-coiled clusters. **Petals:** United into a short tube less than ½" long. **Stems:** Upright, branched, hairy, up to 3' tall. **Leaves:** Alternate, simple, narrowly oblong, without teeth; hairy, up to 7" long. **Season:** March–June. **Habitat:** Sandy soil. **Range** (*see map*): Areas 3–10. **Family:** Forget-me-not. **Comments:** The name refers to the partially coiled clusters of flowers. Rough fiddle head, *A. retrorsa*, has flowers only ¼" long.

Puccoon, *Lithospermum canescens*

Flowers: Up to ½" across, on short, hairy stalks. **Petals:** 5, united below. **Stems:** Upright, often branched, hairy, up to 1½' tall. **Leaves:** Alternate, simple, narrowly oblong, without teeth; softly hairy, up to 1½" long. **Season:** March–June. **Habitat:** Dry woods, prairies, glades. **Range** (*see map*): Areas 1–6, D, E. **Family:** Forget-me-not. **Comments:** This is one of the showiest flowers of prairies and glades. Carolina puccoon, *L. carolinense*, is very similar but has leaves with rough hairs; fringed puccoon, *L. incisum*, has very narrow leaves and short-fringed petals.

Railroad Vine, *Cucurbita foetidissima*

Flowers: Solitary, arising from the leaf axils, up to 4" long and sometimes nearly as wide. **Petals:** 5, united to form a long tube. **Stems:** Creeping, several feet long, with rough hairs. **Leaves:** Alternate, simple, triangular, with angular lobes, toothed; with rough hairs on both surfaces, up to 8" long. **Season:** June–Oct. **Habitat:** Dry, open areas. **Range** (*see map*): Areas 2, 3, 5–8, 10. **Family:** Gourd. **Comments:** This trailing gourd is particularly abundant along railroads in the West. Texas gourd, *C. texana*, has ovate leaves that are not as rough to the touch and flowers less than 3" long.

▲ Yellow Umbrella-plant
  6 separated petal-like parts.
  6–9 stamens.

▲ Fiddle Head
  5 united petals.

▼ Puccoon
  5 united petals.

▼ Railroad Vine
  5 united petals.

RADIAL SYMMETRY

Desert Gold, *Linanthus aureus*

Flowers: Several, in branched terminal clusters, each flower about ½″ across. **Petals:** 5, united into a funnel up to ½″ long. **Stems:** Spreading, much branched, smooth or hairy, up to 4″ tall. **Leaves:** Opposite, divided into 3–7 needle-like lobes; smooth or hairy. **Season:** April–June. **Habitat:** Deserts, sandy soil. **Range** (*see map*): Areas 7, 10. **Family:** Phlox. **Comments:** Bigelow's linanthus, *L. bigelovii*, has yellow flowers about ¾″ long and usually undivided leaves.

Woolly Mullein, *Verbascum thapsus*

Flowers: Crowded on a thick, dense, woolly spike, each flower up to 1″ across. **Petals:** 5, united below. **Stems:** Upright, stout, branched above; with gray, densely woolly hairs; up to 10′ tall. **Leaves:** Basal and alternate, simple, oblong; with gray, densely woolly hairs, the lower leaves up to 12″ long. **Season:** June–Oct. **Habitat:** Open areas. **Range** (*see map*): Areas 1–10, C–F. **Family:** Snapdragon. **Comments:** This is one of the most ubiquitous flowering plants in North America, occurring in all parts of the continent and in most habitats. Moth mullein, *V. blattaria*, is not woolly and usually grows only about 3′ tall; its flowers are not densely crowded into a spike.

Buffalo Bur, *Solanum rostratum*

Flowers: Several, arising from the leaf axils, each flower up to 1¼″ across. **Petals:** 5, united below. **Stems:** Upright, branched, very spiny, up to 1′ tall. **Leaves:** Alternate, deeply cleft with rounded lobes, spiny along the veins. **Season:** June–Oct. **Habitat:** Dry, open areas. **Range** (*see map*): Areas 1–10, C–F. **Family:** Nightshade. **Comments:** The stems and fruits are densely covered with sharp yellow prickles. Another densely prickly species is the southern prickly nightshade, *S. sisymbrifolium*, but it has violet or blue flowers.

Smooth Ground-cherry, *Physalis subglabrata*

Flowers: Solitary, arising from the leaf axils, up to ½″ across; yellow, usually with a brown pattern in the center. **Petals:** 5, united below. **Stems:** Upright, usually smooth, branched, up to 2½′ tall. **Leaves:** Alternate, simple, ovate, wavy-edged or coarsely toothed; smooth. **Season:** July–Sept. **Habitat:** Open areas. **Range** (*see map*): Areas 1–10, E. **Family:** Nightshade. **Comments:** The cherry-like fruit becomes enclosed by the inflated sepals. Long-leaved ground-cherry, *P. longifolia*, has similar flowers but has lanceolate leaves and hairy stems.

▲ Desert Gold
  5 united petals.

▼ Buffalo Bur
  5 united petals.

▲ Woolly Mullein
  5 united petals.

▲ Smooth Ground-cherry
  5 united petals.

YELLOW

BILATERAL SYMMETRY

Hog Potato, *Hoffmanseggia glauca*

Flowers: Several, in elongated clusters, each flower up to ¼" across. **Petals:** Yellow, the upper one speckled with orange. **Stems:** Upright, smooth or hairy, up to 1' tall. **Leaves:** Alternate, divided into 5–11 segments that are further divided into several pairs of leaflets; leaflets are oblong, smooth or hairy, up to ⅓" long. **Season:** March–Sept. **Habitat:** Open areas, particularly along roads. **Range** (*see map*): Areas 5–8, 10. **Family:** Caesalpinia. **Comments:** Rush pea, *H. drepanocarpa*, is very similar but has finely hairy stems and usually fewer flowers.

False Lupine, *Thermopsis montana*

Flowers: Several, in elongated clusters arising from the upper leaf axils, each flower up to 1" long. **Petals:** Bright yellow, forming a pea-shaped flower. **Stems:** Upright, hollow, smooth or nearly so, up to 4' tall. **Leaves:** Alternate, divided into 3 broadly lanceolate leaflets up to 4" long. **Season:** May–Aug. **Habitat:** Meadows, open woods. **Range** (*see map*): Areas 7–9. **Family:** Pea. **Comments:** Although this showy species has the general appearance of a lupine, it has yellow flowers and only 3 leaflets. Golden pea, *T. rhombifolia*, is very similar but stands only 1' tall and has shorter leaflets up to 1½" long.

Yellow Sweet Clover, *Melilotus officinalis*

Flowers: Many, in elongated slender clusters up to 4" long, each flower about ¼" long. **Petals:** Yellow, forming a pea-shaped flower. **Stems:** Upright, branched, smooth, up to 7' tall. **Leaves:** Alternate, divided into 3 leaflets; leaflets are oblong, toothed, smooth or sometimes hairy, up to 1" long. **Season:** June–Sept. **Habitat:** Open areas. **Range** (*see map*): All areas except A. **Family:** Pea. **Comments:** Sweet clovers have a fresh fragrance when cut. They are excellent forage plants for livestock. White sweet clover, *M. alba*, is nearly identical except for its white flowers.

Bird's-foot Trefoil, *Lotus corniculatus*

Flowers: Several, arranged in clusters (umbels), each flower up to ¼" long. **Petals:** Bright yellow, forming a pea-shaped flower. **Stems:** Spreading to upright, smooth or slightly hairy, up to 18" long. **Leaves:** Alternate, divided into 5 leaflets; the leaflets are oblong, smooth or nearly so, up to ½" long. **Season:** June–Sept. **Habitat:** Open areas. **Range** (*see map*): Areas 1–10, C–F. **Family:** Pea. **Comments:** Although several species of *Lotus* occur in North America, the only other widespread one is Pursh's trefoil, *L. purshianus*, a species with pink flowers and 3 leaflets.

▲ Hog Potato
  5 separated petals.

▼ False Lupine
  5 separated petals.
  Pea-shaped flower.

▼ Yellow Sweet Clover
  5 separated petals.
  Pea-shaped flower.

Bird's-foot Trefoil ▶
  5 separated petals.
  Pea-shaped flower.

BILATERAL SYMMETRY

Partridge Pea, *Cassia fasciculata*

Flowers: 2–4, arising from the leaf axils, each flower up to 1½" across. **Petals:** 5, yellow; 3 are slightly smaller than the other 2. **Stems:** Upright, branched, smooth or hairy, up to 2' tall. **Leaves:** Alternate, divided into 20–30 leaflets; each leaflet is narrowly oblong to lanceolate, without teeth, smooth or hairy, up to ¾" long. **Season:** July–Sept. **Habitat:** Fields, prairies, woods, roadsides. **Range** (*see map*): Areas 1–6. **Family:** Caesalpinia. **Comments:** A similar species is sensitive cassia, *C. nictitans*, but it has flowers less than 1" across and up to 40 much narrower leaflets.

Yellow Violet, *Viola pubescens*

Flowers: Solitary, arising from the axils of the upper leaves, each flower up to 1½" long. **Petals:** 5, yellow, sometimes with a few narrow, purple stripes; one of the petals is prolonged backward into a short spur. **Stems:** Upright, smooth or hairy, up to 10" tall. **Leaves:** Basal and alternate, simple, broadly ovate, heart-shaped at the base, toothed; smooth or hairy, up to 2" across. **Season:** March–May. **Habitat:** Shaded woods. **Range** (*see map*): Areas 1–6, D–F. **Family:** Violet. **Comments:** Round-leaved violet, *V. rotundifolia*, is a yellow-flowered species that does not have leafy stems; halberd-leaved violet, *V. hastata*, has yellow flowers and a leafy stem, but the leaves usually have silvery blotches on the upper surface.

Yellow Lady's-slipper Orchid, *Cypripedium calceolus*

Flowers: 1 to a few at the tip of the stem, each flower up to 2½" long, drooping. **Petals:** 3; the lateral 2 are narrow and twisted, the third petal ("lip") is slipper-shaped, up to 2" long. **Stems:** Upright, unbranched, hairy, up to 2' tall. **Leaves:** Alternate, broadly elliptic, hairy, up to 8" long. **Season:** April–May. **Habitat:** Rich woods. **Range** (*see map*): Areas 1–9, D–F. **Family:** Orchid. **Comments:** Other beautiful lady's-slipper orchids include white lady's-slipper, *C. candidum*, with white flowers; showy lady's-slipper, *C. reginae*, with a rose-pink slipper and a leafy stem; and pink moccasin flower, *C. acaule*, with a crimson-pink slipper and only 2 basal leaves.

Yellow Milkwort, *Polygala lutea*

Flowers: Several, crowded into an often spherical head up to 1" across, each flower about ¼" long. **Petal-like Parts:** Have the appearance of 5, not all alike. **Stems:** Upright, smooth, up to 15" tall. **Leaves:** Several crowded at the base of the plant, broadly elliptic, without teeth, up to 2" long; other leaves are alternate along the stem, narrow and smaller. **Season:** June–Aug. **Habitat:** Wet soil. **Range** (*see map*): Areas 1, 2. **Family:** Milkwort. **Comments:** There are more than 50 kinds of milkworts in North America, with pink, purple, white, or yellow flowers. Cymose milkwort, *P. cymosa*, has several elongated heads of yellow flowers.

▲ Yellow Violet
5 separated petals.

▲ Partridge Pea
5 separated petals.

Yellow Milkwort ▶
Appearance of 5 united petal-like parts.
6 stamens.

▼ Yellow Lady's-slipper Orchid
1 pouch-shaped petal. 2 stamens.

BILATERAL SYMMETRY

Dalmatian Toadflax, *Linaria dalmatica*

Flowers: Several, in elongated clusters, each flower up to 2″ long. **Petals:** Strongly 2-lipped, united into a tube and prolonged downward to form a slender spur. **Stems:** Upright, smooth, up to 4′ tall. **Leaves:** Alternate, simple, ovate, without teeth; smooth, up to 3″ long. **Season:** June–Sept. **Habitat:** Open areas. **Range** (*see map*): Areas 1, 3–5, 7–10, C–F. **Family:** Snapdragon. **Comments:** This species is sometimes grown in gardens and escapes from cultivation. Similar is butter-and-eggs, *L. vulgaris*, but its leaves are very narrow.

False Foxglove, *Aureolaria flava*

Flowers: Several, in elongated terminal clusters, each flower up to 2″ long. **Petals:** 5, united below to form a broad tube. **Stems:** Upright, branched, smooth, up to 6′ tall. **Leaves:** Basal leaves are very deeply lobed into many divisions; stem leaves are alternate, less deeply lobed or even without lobes, smooth. **Season:** July–Sept. **Habitat:** Dry woods. **Range** (*see map*): Areas 1–3, 6, E. **Family:** Snapdragon. **Comments:** Large-flowered false foxglove, *A. grandiflora*, is similar but has hairy stems and leaves; smooth false foxglove, *A. laevigata*, has smooth stems, but the leaves are usually undivided.

Yellow Mountain Paintbrush, *Castilleja occidentalis*

Flowers: Several, crowded at the upper end of the plant, each flower up to 1″ long, surrounded by conspicuous yellow leaf-like structures (bracts). **Stems:** Upright, smooth or hairy, up to 8″ tall. **Leaves:** Alternate, simple, narrowly lanceolate, without teeth but occasionally with a pair of lobes; smooth or hairy, up to 2″ long. **Season:** May–July. **Habitat:** High mountains. **Range** (*see map*): Areas 7–9, B, C. **Family:** Snapdragon. **Comments:** Other paintbrushes with yellow bracts are the yellow paintbrush, *C. flava*, with extremely narrow lower leaves; and sulphur paintbrush, *C. sulphurea*, with usually completely smooth stems and leaves.

Yellow Monkey-flower, *Mimulus guttatus*

Flowers: In the axils of the upper leaves, up to 1½″ long. **Petals:** 5, yellow with reddish spots, 2-lipped, united below. **Stems:** Upright, branched, smooth or hairy, up to 3′ tall. **Leaves:** Opposite, simple, ovate, to nearly round, toothed; smooth or hairy, up to 4″ long. **Season:** March–Sept. **Habitat:** Wet soil. **Range** (*see map*): Areas 4, 7–10, A–D. **Family:** Snapdragon. **Comments:** The red-spotted yellow petals and nearly round leaves distinguish this species. Smooth yellow monkey-flower, *M. glabratus*, has creeping stems and smaller flowers.

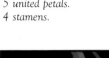
◀ Dalmatian Toadflax
5 united petals.
4 stamens.

▲ False Foxglove
5 united petals.
4 stamens.

▲ Yellow Mountain Paintbrush
5 united petals. 4 stamens.

▲ Yellow Monkey-flower
5 united petals.
4 stamens.

RADIAL SYMMETRY

Copper Iris, *Iris fulva*

Flowers: 1 to a few, up to 4″ across. **Petal-like Parts:** 6, copper-colored, sometimes with green or blue lines. **Stems:** Upright, sometimes branched, up to 3′ tall, bearing the flowers. **Leaves:** Long and arching, smooth, up to 3′ long, less than 1″ wide. **Season:** May–June. **Habitat:** Swampy woods, wet ditches. **Range** (*see map*): Areas 1–3, 6. **Family:** Iris. **Comments:** This very attractive iris is readily distinguished by its copper-colored flowers.

Checker Lily, *Fritillaria lanceolata*

Flowers: Several, nodding, up to 1½″ long, bowl-shaped. **Petal-like Parts:** 6, lanceolate, brownish purple but mottled with green or yellow. **Stems:** Upright, smooth, up to 4′ tall. **Leaves:** Usually in whorls, simple, lanceolate to broadly lanceolate, without teeth; smooth, up to 4″ long. **Season:** Feb–June. **Habitat:** Open woods, grassy areas. **Range** (*see map*): Areas 9, 10, C. **Family:** Lily. **Comments:** This striking species is also known as mission bells. Another similar checker lily, *F. atropurpurea*, has flowers only ¾″ long; chocolate lily, *F. biflora*, has dark brown flowers without any mottling; Kamchatka lily, *F. camschatcensis*, has deep purple-brown flowers.

Red Trillium, *Trillium recurvatum*

Flowers: Solitary, above the cluster of leaves, up to 1½″ long, not borne on a stalk. **Petals:** 3, maroon, separated. **Stems:** Upright, unbranched, smooth, up to 18″ tall. **Leaves:** 3 in a whorl just beneath the flower, oval to ovate, without teeth; often mottled, smooth, up to 4″ long, on a distinct stalk. **Season:** March–May. **Habitat:** Rich woods. **Range** (*see map*): Areas 1–3, 6. **Family:** Lily. **Comments:** This species is sometimes called wake robin. A similar species is sessile trillium, *T. sessile*, but its leaves do not have stalks.

Wild Ginger, *Asarum canadense*

Flowers: Solitary, between 2 basal leaves, each flower up to 1″ across. **Petals:** None, but the 3 sepals are petal-like, united below, maroon-purple. **Stems:** All below ground. **Leaves:** Usually 2, opposite, borne near the ground, ovate, heart-shaped; hairy, up to 6″ long. **Season:** April–May. **Habitat:** Rich woods. **Range** (*see map*): Areas 1–5, D–F. **Family:** Birthwort. **Comments:** The underground stems can be used as a source for ginger. The 3 petal-like sepals vary in shape in different parts of the country. Western wild ginger, *A. caudatum*, has each sepal prolonged into a tail up to 2″ long.

▲ Copper Iris
  6 petal-like parts.

Checker Lily ▶
  6 petal-like parts.

▲ Red Trillium
  3 separated petals.

Wild Ginger ▶
  3 united petal-like parts.

RADIAL SYMMETRY

Blue Cohosh, *Caulophyllum thalictroides*

Flowers: Several to many, in terminal clusters, each flower up to ½" across. **Petals:** 6, separated, greenish or yellow-green, shorter than the 6 oblong green sepals. **Stems:** Upright, smooth, bluish, up to 3' tall. **Leaves:** Usually 1 near the top of the stem and 1 near the bottom; each leaf is divided into 3 oval to oblong, coarsely toothed, smooth leaflets. **Season:** March–June. **Habitat:** Rich woods. **Range** (*see map*): Areas 1–5, D–F. **Family:** Barberry. **Comments:** The spherical blue fruits, which follow the flowers, are poisonous.

Spider Antelope Horns, *Asclepias asperula*

Flowers: Several, in terminal clusters (umbels), each flower up to 1½" across. **Petals:** 5, pale yellow-green, sometimes with a purple tinge, up to ½" long, each with a low, dark red-purple hood above it. **Stems:** Clustered at base, upright or spreading, unbranched, hairy, with milky sap, up to 1½' tall. **Leaves:** More or less alternate, simple, narrowly lanceolate, without teeth; hairy, with milky sap. **Season:** March–Aug. **Habitat:** Open areas. **Range** (*see map*): Areas 5–8, 10. **Family:** Milkweed. **Comments:** Green antelope horns, *A. viridis*, is similar but has smooth, broader leaves.

Tall Green Milkweed, *Asclepias hirtella*

Flowers: Several, in clusters (umbels) at the end of the stem or arising from the leaf axils; each flower is hourglass-shaped, up to ¼" long, borne on hairy stalks. **Petals:** 5, greenish, turned downward. **Stems:** Upright, usually unbranched, hairy, with milky sap, up to 3' tall. **Leaves:** Usually alternate, simple, narrowly lanceolate, without teeth; hairy, with milky sap, up to ½" wide. **Season:** May–Aug. **Habitat:** Prairies, fields. **Range** (*see map*): Areas 1–3, 5, 6, E. **Family:** Milkweed. **Comments:** Narrow-leaved green milkweed, *A. stenophylla*, has similar flowers but very narrow leaves less than ¼" wide.

Monument Plant, *Frasera speciosa*

Flowers: Several, in clusters arising from the axils of the upper leaves, each flower up to 1½" across. **Petals:** 4, united at the base, green or yellow-green with small purple spots, each petal with 2 hairy glands. **Stems:** Upright, smooth, up to 7' tall. **Leaves:** In whorls of 3 or 4; the basal leaves are lanceolate, without teeth, smooth, up to 20" long; the upper leaves are similar but smaller. **Season:** May–Aug. **Habitat:** Open woods. **Range** (*see map*): Areas 4, 6–10. **Family:** Gentian. **Comments:** This species is also called deer's ears, because of the fancied resemblance of the leaves to the ears of deer. American columbo, *F. caroliniensis*, has a single hairy gland on each petal; star swertia, *Swertia perennis*, usually has 5 blue-purple petals.

▲ Blue Cohosh
  6 separated petals.

▲ Spider Antelope Horns
  5 petals. Milky sap.

▲ Tall Green Milkweed
  5 petals. Milky sap.

Monument Plant ▶
4 united petals.

PETALS ABSENT

Skunk Cabbage, *Symplocarpus foetidus*

Flowers: Many, crowded on a 1″ thick, fleshy structure (spadix), partially enclosed by a modified leaf (spathe) that is purple-brown to greenish yellow; the spathe is up to 6″ long and 3″ wide. **Petals:** None. **Stems:** Underground. **Leaves:** Several, basal, without teeth; smooth, up to 2½′ long, up to nearly 1′ wide; produced after the plant flowers. **Season:** Feb–May. **Habitat:** Wet woods. **Range** (*see map*): Areas 1–3, E, F. **Family:** Aroid. **Comments:** This bizarre plant has a putrid odor combining skunk with onion. Despite this, the roots contain starch and have been used in making bread. Western skunk cabbage, *Lysichiton americanum*, has a yellow spathe up to 8″ long and leaves up to 5′ long.

Common Cat-tail, *Typha latifolia*

Flowers: Crowded together into dense terminal cylindrical spikes. **Petals:** None. **Stems:** Upright, robust, smooth, up to 9′ tall. **Leaves:** Several, flat, very long, up to 1½″ wide. **Season:** May–July. **Habitat:** Marshes, shallow water. **Range** (*see map*): All areas. **Family:** Cat-tail. **Comments:** Narrow-leaved cat-tail, *T. angustifolia*, differs by its more slender flowering spikes and its fewer, narrower leaves.

Jack-in-the-pulpit, *Arisaema triphyllum*

Flowers: Very small, crowded together at the lower end of a cylindrical column (spadix), overtopped by an arching modified leaf (spathe). **Petals:** None. **Stems:** Underground. **Leaves:** 1, basal, divided into 3 leaflets; the leaflets are ovate to lanceolate, without teeth, smooth. **Season:** March–May. **Habitat:** Woods. **Range** (*see map*): Areas 1–6, D–F. **Family:** Aroid. **Comments:** The spathes may be solid green or green with purple stripes. The underground roots, known as Indian turnips, contain microscopic pointed crystals that render them too sharp to be eaten unless boiled. Green dragon, *A. dracontium*, has a tail-like spadix that protrudes above the spathe; its leaves are divided into 5–17 leaflets.

Bur-reed, *Sparganium eurycarpum*

Flowers: Crowded into spherical green heads up to 1¼″ in diameter. **Petals:** None. **Stems:** Upright, sparsely branched, smooth, up to 4′ tall. **Leaves:** Alternate, simple, long and narrow, without teeth; smooth. **Season:** July–Sept. **Habitat:** Shallow water, marshes. **Range** (*see map*): Areas 1–10, C–F. **Family:** Bur-reed. **Comments:** The fruits of this and other bur-reeds are eaten by waterfowl.

▲ Skunk Cabbage
No petals.

▲ Common Cat-tail
No petals.

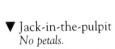

▼ Jack-in-the-pulpit
No petals.

▼ Bur-reed
No petals.

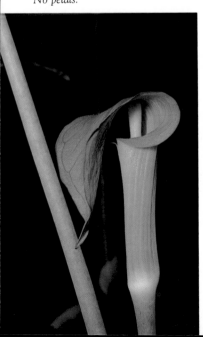

Families of Flowering Plants

Acanthus Family, Acanthaceae

Although this is generally a tropical family, nearly 100 species occur naturally in North America north of Mexico. Most of them are perennial wildflowers, although the family also includes a few shrubs. The acanthus family is distinguished by a combination of characters: five petals (often two-lipped) united below to form a tube, four stamens, and seeds attached to special short, curved, hardened stalks. Blue is the predominant flower color. Members of this family usually have opposite, simple leaves without teeth or lobes. The dry fruits usually split into three parts when the seeds are ripe. Some of the common genera in eastern North America are wild petunia (*Ruellia*) and water willow (*Justicia*). Genera found in the Southwest include scaly-stems (*Elytraria*), *Carlowrightia*, and *Stenandrium*. The climbing clockvine, *Thunbergia alata*, is a popular ornamental.

Aroid Family, Araceae

Essentially a tropical group, this family has a unique arrangement of its flowers. The minute flowers are crowded together on an elongated stalk that botanists term a spadix. A leafy structure called a sheath usually encloses or arches over the spadix. Jack-in-the-pulpit is a good example. Each flower lacks petals and usually has tiny stamens and pistils. Many aroids, particularly tropical species, are noted for their handsome leaves. Common cultivated examples are philodendrons, monsteras, anthuriums, calla lilies, elephant's ears, Chinese evergreens, dieffenbachias, and caladiums. Native North American aroids include jack-in-the-pulpit and green dragon (*Arisaema*), eastern skunk cabbage (*Symplocarpus*), western skunk cabbage (*Lysichiton*), sweet flag (*Acorus*), arrow arum (*Peltandra*), and golden spike (*Orontium*). About three dozen species occur in the wild in North America.

Aster Family, Asteraceae

The aster family is the largest family of flowering plants in North America and one with extremely complex flower structures. More than 2,500 different species of this family grow wild on this continent. Their diversity is staggering, and the range of appearance of the flowers is difficult to believe. Ragweeds, with tiny, inconspicuous, green flowers are in the same family as the annual sunflower, with its large, showy heads. There is one characteristic, however, that unites all members of the aster family as a unit. What appears to be a single flower, such as the head of a sunflower, is actually many flowers crowded together and sharing a common axis;

botanists call this head to which the flowers are attached a receptacle. Each yellow ray of a sunflower is a single flower, and each unit in the dark center is a single flower. One sunflower head thus may consist of several hundred flowers, and a ragweed head may consist of only a few; both are alike in that the flowers share a common receptacle.

Variation in the family comes from the different types of flowers that make up the head. The sunflower head is a good example. Each yellow petal-like structure is a ray flower. It often has tiny teeth or notches at its tip. At the base of each ray there is often a tiny pistil with a style and two-part stigma emerging from its summit. There may or may not be tiny stamens associated with the ray flower. The center of a sunflower is referred to as a disk, and it is composed of several or more tiny, elongated, tubular flowers called disk flowers. Each disk flower is usually divided at its tip into five lobes. At the bottom of many disk flowers is the pistil. Again, stamens may be produced by a disk flower.

The sunflower has both disk flowers and ray flowers; bachelor's buttons have only disk flowers; dandelions have only ray flowers. Those plants that produce only ray flowers also have milky sap in their stems and leaves; the others do not. In every case, however, the pistils develop into tiny, hard, single-seeded fruits. Often, a tuft of hairs, called the pappus, is attached to the upper end of the fruit and serves as a parachute during seed dispersal.

Only a small fraction of the wild members of the aster family are covered in this book. Many species in the family are cultivated in gardens because of their handsome flowers. These include chrysanthemums, daisies, sunflowers, asters, marigolds, zinnias, cosmos, coreopsis, cinerarias, dahlias, gerberas, tansy, straw flowers, and edelweiss. Some members of the family are edible, such as artichokes, lettuce, endive, and salsify.

Barberry Family, Berberidaceae

Although the barberry family is relatively small (about 200 species worldwide and 32 in North America), it is surprisingly diverse. Some, like barberries and Oregon grapes, are shrubs; others, like mayapples, are herbs. Members of this family have either alternate or basal leaves that are simple or pinnately compound. In most genera, there are from four to six petals per flower and a like number of stamens. The petals and sepals are entirely free from each other. A single pistil completes the flower. Wildflowers in North America include mayapple (*Podophyllum*), blue cohosh (*Caulophyllum*), twinleaf (*Jeffersonia*), umbrella-leaf (*Diphylleia*), deerfoot (*Achlys*), and the unusual inside-out flowers (*Vancouveria*).

Birthwort Family, Aristolochiaceae

The six genera and more than 400 species in the birthwort family are mostly found in the tropics; only three genera and fewer than three dozen species grow wild in North America. The family includes high climbing vines, such as dutchman's pipevine (*Aristolochia*), and low-growing herbs, such as wild ginger (*Asarum*). The family is distinguished by its flowers, which lack petals and have the stamens and style attached to each other.

Bur-reed Family, Sparganiaceae

Sparganium is the only member of this family, and it is found throughout the world in temperate and frigid regions. In North America there are only nine species. Each of these lives in or near water and has large bur-like heads of pistil-bearing flowers and smaller heads of pollen-bearing flowers. All the flowers lack petals.

Buttercup Family, Ranunculaceae

The buttercup family is most prevalent in cooler regions of the Northern Hemisphere. Altogether there are about 2,000 species in this family, all of them herbs. More than 300 grow wild in North America. Distinguishing field marks include compound leaves and many stamens and pistils in a single flower. Among the most prominent genera are buttercups (*Ranunculus*), columbines (*Aquilegia*), larkspurs (*Delphinium*), windflowers (*Anemone*), globe flowers (*Trollius*), hellebores (*Helleborus*), monkshoods (*Aconitum*), goldenseals (*Hydrastis*), hepaticas (*Hepatica*), marsh marigolds (*Caltha*), black cohoshes (*Cimicifuga*), and the sometimes viny clematis (*Clematis*).

Cactus Family, Cactaceae

Almost every one of the 2,000 kinds of wild cacti in the world occur naturally in the Americas, with nearly 200 of them native to North America north of Mexico. Cacti are readily recognized by their succulent, or fleshy, stems, which usually have spines in place of broad, flat leaves. The water-storing capability of the stems and the absence of regular leaves help cacti to survive in regions where moisture is scarce. Cactus flowers are usually showy and consist of many free petals and many stamens.

Caesalpinia Family, Caesalpiniaceae

The caesalpinia family is most common in the tropics, where it has as many as 2,000 species of trees, shrubs, vines, and herbs. In North America, about 75 species may be found. Most of these are either caesalpinias (*Caesalpinia*) or sennas (*Cassia*), although a few small genera also occur, including hog peanut (*Hoffmanseggia*), redbud (*Cercis*), coffee tree (*Gymnocladus*), honey locust (*Gleditsia*), and paloverde (*Parkinsonia*). The family is distinguished by its alternate, compound leaves (except redbud) and its bilaterally symmetrical flowers with five free petals of unequal size and ten stamens. The beautiful poinciana (*Delonix*) and the edible tamarind (*Tamarindus*) and St. John's-bread (*Ceratonia*) belong to this family.

Caper Family, Capparidaceae

Only 43 species of the caper family grow in North America, only a small percentage of the family's total of 700 species, found primarily in the tropics. Most of those in North America are herbs, but shrubs, trees, and even high-climbing vines grow in the tropics. Distinguishing field characters for this family include the bilaterally symmetrical flowers, often four free petals, and four or more stamens. Genera include spider-flowers (*Cleome*), capers (*Capparis*), and jackass clover (*Wislizenia*).

Carrot Family, Apiaceae

The carrot family is found throughout the Northern Hemisphere, where there are more than 3,000 different species. In North America alone, there are nearly 400 species. All are herbs, and most of them have aromatic leaves. The chief characteristic that distinguishes this family is the arrangement of the flowers in umbels. Each flower has five free petals and five stamens. The family includes carrot (*Daucus*), parsnip (*Pastinaca*), eryngo (*Eryngium*), water hemlock (*Cicuta*), poison hemlock (*Conium*), cow parsnip (*Heracleum*), chervil (*Chaerophyllum*), and snakeroot (*Sanicula*).

Cat-tail Family, Typhaceae

Cat-tails are large, marsh-inhabiting herbs found throughout most of the world. There is a total of 15 species in the world, five of which occur in North America north of Mexico. The tiny flowers are crowded into cylindrical spikes. The pollen-producing flowers are located in slender spikes that are situated immediately above the thicker and darker-colored spikes that contain the pistil-forming flowers. *Typha* is the only genus.

Diapensia Family, Diapensiaceae

There are only six genera and ten species in this family, found in the cooler and arctic regions of the Northern Hemisphere. There are four genera and four species in North America. The family is distinguished by its five united petals and five stamens that are attached to the petals.

Dogbane Family, Apocynaceae

Most of the 1,300 species in this family are tropical, with only about 75 found in North America north of Mexico. In this family are herbs, shrubs, trees, and vines. Many of them have milky sap. Other field marks include simple, toothless leaves, five united petals, and five stamens. Representative genera in North America include dogbane (*Apocynum*), bluestar (*Amsonia*), and periwinkle (*Vinca*). Oleander (*Nerium*) and frangipani (*Plumeria*) are two woody genera that are often planted in warmer parts of North America.

Dogwood Family, Cornaceae

Except for bunchberry and the boreal dogwood, the other 90 members of the dogwood family are either trees, shrubs, or woody vines. Some of our most attractive flowering trees are dogwoods. The family in North America consists of about 15 species, almost all with opposite, simple, toothless leaves and four-part flowers.

Evening Primrose Family, Onagraceae

More than one-third of the 640 species in the evening primrose family occur in North America, with the majority of them living in the western half of the continent. Most are herbs and are readily distinguished by their four separated petals and simple leaves. Showy wildflowers in the family include evening primroses (*Oenothera*), fireweeds (*Epilobium*), water primroses (*Ludwigia*), beeblossoms (*Gaura*), clarkias (*Clarkia*), brown eyes and yellow cups (*Camissonia*), western sundrops (*Calylophus*), gayophytums (*Gayophytum*), and enchanter's nightshades (*Circaea*). A commonly grown ornamental is fuchsia (*Fuchsia*).

Flax Family, Linaceae

The approximately 200 species in the flax family occur in temperate regions of the world. Of these, 48 grow in North America north of Mexico. Most of them are herbs with simple, toothless leaves. Their flowers are radially symmetrical and have five separated petals and usually five stamens with united bases. Most North American species belong to one of two genera: *Linum* and *Hesperolinon*.

Forget-me-not Family, Boraginaceae

The forget-me-not family, with a total of about 2,000 species, is found both in the tropics and in temperate regions of the world. Many of the tropical members of the family are trees, and most of the temperate species are herbaceous wildflowers. The distinguishing features of the family are the alternate leaves, five united petals, five stamens, and a four-part ovary. Representative plants in this family are forget-me-nots (*Myosotis*), bluebells (*Mertensia*), heliotropes (*Heliotropium*), puccoons (*Lithospermum*), popcorn flowers (*Plagiobothrys*), cryptanthas (*Cryptantha*), and hound's-tongues (*Cynoglossum*).

Four-o'clock Family, Nyctaginaceae

The 250 species of the four-o'clock family are scattered throughout much of the American tropics and subtropics. More than 100 grow in North America north of Mexico. Most members of the family are distinguished by the brightly colored leaf-like structures (bracts) that surround the flowers. In addition to four-o'clocks (*Mirabilis*), the family also contains sand verbenas (*Abronia*) and angel trumpets (*Acleisanthes*). Bougainvillea (*Bougainvillea*) is a popular ornamental in warm climates.

Gentian Family, Gentianaceae

The gentian family is of worldwide distribution, with about 800 species, found mostly in temperate regions. Almost all are herbaceous wildflowers with radially symmetrical flowers that have five united petals and the same number of stamens attached to them. The 117 North American species include gentians (*Gentiana*), prairie gentians (*Eustoma*), marsh pinks (*Sabatia*), and centauries (*Centaurium*).

Geranium Family, Geraniaceae

The temperate and tropical regions of the world are home to more than 800 species of the geranium family. Most of them are herbaceous wildflowers with compound or deeply lobed leaves, five free petals, and fruits with slender beaks. There are 60 species in North America north of Mexico. Most of them are either geraniums or crane's-bills (*Geranium*) or stork's-bills (*Erodium*).

Gourd Family, Cucurbitaceae

Most of the 850 wild species in the gourd family live in the tropics and subtropics. About 75 are found in North America north of Mexico. Most gourds are creeping or climbing plants, and most bear tendrils. The flowers have five united petals. American genera include squirting cucumbers (*Echinocystis* and *Melothria*), bur cucumbers (*Sicyos*), globeberries (*Ibervillea*), and gourds (*Cucurbita*).

Harebell Family, Campanulaceae

The harebell family, with about 600 species, is widely distributed in the temperate regions of the world. In North America, about 55 species may be found growing without cultivation. Most of them are recognized by their alternate, simple leaves and their radially symmetrical flowers with five united petals and five stamens. The best known wildflowers are bellflowers and harebells (*Campanula*), Venus' looking glasses (*Triodanis*), blue cups (*Githopsis*), sheep's-bits (*Jasione*), and wahlenbergias (*Wahlenbergia*).

Indian Pipe Family, Monotropaceae

The Indian pipe family, unique because it lacks chlorophyll and has no green members, is confined to temperate and boreal regions of the Northern Hemisphere. There are 13 species in North America. In addition to the absence of green leaves, these species usually have flowers with four or five waxy petals and eight or ten stamens. North American genera include Indian pipes (*Monotropa*), pinedrops (*Pterospora*), sugarsticks (*Allotropa*), and snow plants (*Sarcodes*).

Iris Family, Iridaceae

Although there are approximately 1,500 species in the iris family, distributed over much of the world, only about 100 of them grow wild in North America. They are readily distinguished by their narrow, sword-like leaves and flower parts that are usually arranged in multiples of 3. In addition to the widespread irises (*Iris*), other genera include blue-eyed-grass (*Sisyrin-*

chium) and nemastylis (*Nemastylis*). Crocus, gladiolus, and freesia are commonly cultivated members of the iris family.

Jewelweed Family, Balsaminaceae

Most of the 450 species of the jewelweed family live in the tropics of Asia and Africa. Only two species of touch-me-nots (*Impatiens*) are found with any regularity in North America. They are recognized by their strongly bilaterally symmetrical flowers with a curved spur, nearly transparent stems, and fruits that burst open when touched.

Lily Family, Liliaceae

The lily family, known to many because several species have showy flowers, consists of about 4,000 species found in temperate and tropical regions of the world. Nearly 500 species occur in North America north of Mexico. Most of them are recognized by their flowers, which have six petal-like parts and six stamens. The leaves usually have parallel veins. Many genera of wildflowers in the lily family occur in North America, including wild lilies (*Lilium*), trout lilies (*Erythronium*), wild hyacinths (*Camassia*), bro-diaeas (*Brodiaea*), solomon's seals (*Polygonatum*) false solomon's seals (*Smilacina*), star tulips and cat's-ears (*Calochortus*), fritillaries (*Fritillaria*), twisted-stalks (*Streptopus*), golden bellflowers (*Uvularia*), death camas (*Zigadenus*), trilliums (*Trillium*), star-grasses (*Hypoxis*), spider lilies (*Hymenocallis*), wild onions (*Allium*), and zephyr lilies (*Zephyranthes*).

Lizard's Tail Family, Saururaceae

This is one of the smallest families of flowering plants in the world, with only four known species. Two of these occur in North America. One is lizard's tail (*Saururus*), from the eastern part of the continent; the other is yerba mansa (*Anemopsis*), from the West. Although the members of this family lack petals, they usually are showy because of their bright white stamens or large, white leaf-like structures (bracts).

Lobelia Family, Lobeliaceae

The 700 species that belong to the lobelia family are found mostly in the tropics, although about 50 species occur in North America north of Mexico. Most of them have bilaterally symmetrical flowers with five united petals and five stamens. In addition to lobelias (*Lobelia*), the family includes downingias (*Downingia*) and thread plants (*Nemacladus*).

Logania Family, Loganiaceae

Although the logania family consists of about 500 mostly woody species that live in the tropics, a few showy species do grow wild in North America.

Best known are Indian pinks (*Spigelia*) and the climbing yellow jessamine (*Gelsemium*). The family is usually distinguished by its opposite leaves and often five united petals with five stamens. Strychnine trees (*Strychnos*), found in the tropics, also belong to this family.

Loosestrife Family, Lythraceae

The American tropics abound with members of the loosestrife family, with nearly 400 species represented. In North America north of Mexico, there are only 29 wild species. Their flowers usually have four or six free petals and twice the number of stamens. Native genera include loosestrifes (*Lythrum*), water loosestrifes (*Decodon*), and clammy weeds (*Cuphaea*). The most popular ornamental is crepe myrtle (*Lagerstroemia*).

Madder Family, Rubiaceae

The madder family is the fifth largest family of flowering plants in the world, with more than 5,000 species. Many of these are found in the tropics and take the form of trees and shrubs. Nearly 175 species grow in North America north of Mexico. Most of these temperate species are herbaceous wildflowers. Among them are bluets (*Hedyotis*), bedstraws (*Galium*), partridge-berry (*Mitchella*), buttonweeds (*Diodia*), bouvardias (*Bouvardia*), and the shrubby buttonbush (*Cephalanthus*). The family has simple, opposite leaves with tiny leaves or bristles (stipules) where the leaves are attached to the stem. The four or five petals of the radially symmetrical flowers are united. There are four or five stamens. Other familiar members of the madder family are coffee (*Coffea*), gardenias (*Gardenia*), quinine tree (*Cinchona*), and ixoras (*Ixora*).

Mallow Family, Malvaceae

The American tropics are home to a large number of the 1,500 species that make up the mallow family. Nearly 200 species grow in North America north of Mexico. The major distinguishing field marks are the numerous united stamens, which form a conspicuous central column. The radially symmetrical flower also has five separated petals. Genera include velvet-leaf (*Abutilon*), mallows (*Malva*), globe mallows (*Sphaeralcea*), checker mallows (*Sidalcea*), poppy mallows '(*Callirhoe*), hibiscus (*Hibiscus*), holly-hocks (*Alcea*), and cotton (*Gossypium*). The vegetable called okra (*Abelmoschus*) also belongs to the mallow family.

Martynia Family, Martyniaceae

The martynia family is a warm-climate family with only 16 species. Nine of them grow in North America, most of them known as unicorn plants (*Martynia*). In addition to the unusually curved, hooked beaks on the fruits, which account for the name unicorn, the family has bilaterally symmetrical flowers with five petals united into a tube and four stamens attached to the tube. Most of them have opposite, simple leaves.

Meadow Beauty Family, Melastomaceae

Almost all of the 4,000 species of the meadow beauty family live in the tropics. Only 12 members of this family grow in North America north of Mexico, all but one of them meadow beauties (*Rhexia*). The family is easily recognized by its opposite, simple leaves, which have strong parallel vein patterns, and its eight or ten stamens, which are conspicuously jointed. There are usually four or five separated petals.

Milkweed Family, Asclepiadaceae

This is primarily a tropical and subtropical family with about 2,000 species. Only about 125 occur in North America north of Mexico. They are usually recognized by their opposite leaves, milky sap, radially symmetrical flowers with five petals, and two ovaries in each flower. The common American genera are milkweeds (*Asclepias*) and climbing milkweeds (*Cynanchum*, *Gonolobus*, and *Matelea*).

Milkwort Family, Polygalaceae

The 700 species that belong to the milkwort family are scattered throughout most parts of the world except the coldest regions. Fifty-six occur in North America, all but one of them in the genus *Polygala*. The family is distinguished by its unusual bilaterally symmetrical flower, which has five sepals (two of them usually petal-like), three petals, and eight stamens.

Mint Family, Lamiaceae

Most of the world's 3,200 mints occur in temperate climates, with the greatest number found around the Mediterranean Sea. Nearly 400 species occur in North America. The family is readily recognized by its square stems; opposite, simple leaves; and bilaterally symmetrical flowers with five united petals, two or four stamens, and a four-part ovary. Many genera occur in this continent including sages (*Salvia*), pagoda plants (*Blephilia*), skullcaps (*Scutellaria*), dragon's-heads (*Dracocephalum*), false dragon's-heads (*Physostegia*), water horehounds (*Lycopus*), mints (*Mentha*), self-heals (*Prunella*), mountain mints (*Pycnanthemum*), hedeomas (*Hedeoma*), hedge nettles (*Stachys*), germanders (*Teucrium*), and beebalms (*Monarda*).

Morning Glory Family, Convolvulaceae

There are more than 1,500 members of the morning glory family, found primarily in tropical and subtropical regions, but about 110 species range into North America north of Mexico. Most species on this continent are twining vines, often with milky sap. The flowers are radially symmetrical, with five petals united to form tubes or funnels. There are five stamens. Common plants are morning glories (*Ipomoea*) and bindweeds (*Convolvulus* and *Calystegia*).

Mustard Family, Brassicaceae

One of the easiest families to recognize in the field is the mustard family. The flowers are radially symmetrical, with four separated petals and six stamens. The leaves are alternate. The family comprises about 3,200 species, most of them in the Northern Hemisphere. More than 600 are in North America. There are many common genera, including yellow rockets (*Barbarea*), wild mustards (*Brassica*), rock cresses (*Arabis*), whitlow worts (*Draba*), bladderpods (*Lesquerella*), peppergrasses (*Lepidium*), penny cresses (*Thlaspi*), bitter cresses (*Cardamine*), twinpods (*Physaria*), jewelflowers (*Streptanthus*), hedge mustards (*Sisymbrium*), wallflowers (*Erysimum*), tansy mustards (*Descurainia*), and yellow cresses (*Rorippa*).

Nightshade Family, Solanaceae

There are more than 2,000 species in the nightshade family, the greatest percentage of them in tropical Central America and South America. About 150 grow wild in North America. Most of them have radially symmetrical flowers with five united petals and five stamens. Common representatives are nightshades (*Solanum*), ground-cherries (*Physalis*), wild tobaccos (*Nicotiana*), jimson-weeds (*Datura*), and matrimony vines (*Lycium*). Other well-known genera are petunias (*Petunia*) and tomatoes (*Lycopersicon*).

Orchid Family, Orchidaceae

The orchid family is the largest of all families of flowering plants, with more than 17,000 species. Most of them are found in the tropics, where many grow on other plants as epiphytes. Nearly 200 occur in North America north of Mexico. The flower structure sets the orchids apart. There are three sepals and three petals. One of the petals (the "lip") is always different in shape from the other two. There are only one or two stamens. Genera include lady's-slippers (*Cypripedium*), calypsos (*Calypso*), twayblades (*Liparis*), coral-roots (*Corallorhiza*), lady's-tresses (*Spiranthes*), pogonias (*Pogonia* and *Calopogon*), habenarias (*Habenaria* and *Platanthera*), rattlesnake orchids (*Goodyera*), and adder's-mouth orchids (*Malaxis*).

Passion-flower Family, Passifloraceae

Most members of the passion-flower family are vines with tendrils. Their flowers are among the most intricate in the world. In addition to the usually five sepals and five petals are numerous petal-like accessory structures that make up the corona. Although there are more than 600 species in this family, found mostly in the tropics, only 14 occur in North America. All belong to the genus *Passiflora*.

Pea Family, Papilionaceae

Although the 10,000-member pea family is best developed in the tropics, nearly 1,500 species occur in North America. They may be trees, shrubs, herbs, or vines. Most have pea-shaped flowers that consist of two lateral petals (wings), a larger back petal (standard), and a ridged petal (keel) that faces the standard. The leaves are alternate and compound. Representative genera include clovers (*Trifolium*), sweet clovers (*Melilotus*), prairie clovers (*Dalea*), lupines (*Lupinus*), baptisias (*Baptisia*), rattleboxes (*Crotalaria*), bird's-foot trefoils (*Lotus*), scurf peas (*Psoralea*), wisterias (*Wisteria*), locusts (*Robinia*), mesquites (*Sophora*), milk vetches (*Astragalus*), locoweeds (*Oxytropis*), vetches (*Vicia*), crown vetches (*Coronilla*), tick trefoils (*Desmodium*), bush clovers (*Lespedeza*), sweet peas (*Lathyrus*), ground nuts (*Apios*), milk peas (*Galactia*), and wild beans (*Phaseolus*).

Phlox Family, Polemoniaceae

Almost all of the 300 species in the phlox family occur in North America, with the majority of them in the West. The family is readily distinguished by its radially symmetrical flowers with five petals united to form a tube, five stamens, and three stigmas. In addition to phloxes (*Phlox*), the family includes gilias (*Gilia*), desert trumpets (*Ipomopsis*), baby stars (*Linanthus*), collomias (*Collomia*), polemoniums (*Polemonium*), langloisias (*Langloisia*), wool stars (*Eriastrum*), and navarretias (*Navarretia*).

Pickerelweed Family, Pontederiaceae

There are 28 fresh-water aquatic species in this family; nine of them occur in North America. The members of this family are distinguished by their bilaterally symmetrical flowers with six petal-like parts. Representative genera are pickerelweeds (*Pontederia*), water hyacinths (*Eichhornia*), and mud plantains (*Heteranthera*).

Pink Family, Caryophyllaceae

The pink family is a family of temperate regions of the world. Of the 2,100 species, nearly 300 occur in North America. All of them have opposite, simple, toothless leaves and radially symmetrical flowers with five free petals. Genera include chickweeds (*Stellaria*), mouse-eared chickweeds (*Cerastium*), catchflys (*Silene*), evening campions (*Lychnis*), corn cockles (*Agrostemma*), sandworts (*Arenaria*), bouncing bets (*Saponaria*), pearlworts (*Sagina*), and pinks (*Dianthus*).

Pitcher Plant Family, Sarraceniaceae

Except for a small number of species in the mountains of northern South America, the pitcher plant family is native to bogs in North America. There are eight species of pitcher plants (*Sarracenia*) in the eastern United States, and one cobra plant (*Darlingtonia*) in Oregon and California. Some of the leaves are modified into pitchers that trap insects. Unable to escape from the pitcher, the insect dies, and its body is broken down by the plant's digestive enzymes. The flowers of the pitcher plants have five free petals that surround a broadly expanded, umbrella-like style (the stalk-like part of the pistil that joins ovary and stigma).

Pokeweed Family, Phytolaccaceae

Most of the 125 species in the pokeweed family live in the American tropics; eight species grow in North America. Distinguishing features of this family are the alternate, simple, toothless leaves and the five petal-like sepals. Pokeweed (*Phytolacca*) and pigeon-berry (*Rivina*) are the best known genera.

Poppy Family, Papaveraceae

There are about 700 species in the poppy family, most of them found in temperate regions of the Northern Hemisphere; 84 occur in North America. Although the plants that make up the family are diverse, most of them have four petals and six or more stamens. The leaves are alternate and often much-divided. Genera in North America are poppies (*Papaver*), celandine poppy (*Stylophorum*), california poppies (*Eschscholtzia*), prickly poppies (*Argemone*), bloodroots (*Sanguinaria*), fumitories (*Corydalis*), and bleeding hearts and dutchman's breeches (*Dicentra*).

Portulaca Family, Portulacaceae

Members of the portulaca family usually have bilaterally symmetrical flowers with only two sepals, separated petals, and an ovary with from two to five styles (the stalk-like part of the pistil that joins ovary and stigma). There are more than 500 species worldwide, with 90 of them found in North America. Representative genera are spring beauties (*Claytonia*), purslanes (*Portulaca*), lewisias (*Lewisia*), montias (*Montia*), flowers-of-an-hour (*Talinum*), red maids (*Calandrinia*), and pussy paws (*Calyptridium*).

Primrose Family, Primulaceae

Although the primrose family is found in all parts of the world, it is most abundant in north temperate regions. Of the 800 species known, about 80 occur in North America. They are readily distinguished by their usually five united petals and five stamens. Best-known genera are primroses (*Primula*), shooting stars (*Dodecatheon*), yellow loosestrifes (*Lysimachia*), pimpernels (*Anagallis*), star-flowers (*Trientalis*), and douglasias (*Douglasia*).

Pyrola Family, Pyrolaceae

Only about 20 species make up the pyrola family, and all of them are found in boreal and temperate regions of the Northern Hemisphere. Their flowers have five free petals and ten stamens. All North American species are either wintergreens (*Chimaphila*) or pyrolas (*Pyrola*).

Rose Family, Rosaceae

This large and diverse family consists of about 2,000 species of trees, shrubs, and herbs distributed over much of the earth. More than 800 occur in North America. Most members of the family have radially symmetrical flowers and five free petals, but few other characteristics can be named to distinguish them. Among the many genera are roses (*Rosa*), hawthorns (*Crataegus*), blackberries (*Rubus*), strawberries (*Fragaria*), apples (*Malus*), cherries and plums (*Prunus*), shadbushes (*Amelanchier*), mountain ashes (*Sorbus*), avens (*Geum*), cinquefoils (*Potentilla*), spiraeas (*Spiraea*), and agrimonies (*Agrimonia*).

Saxifrage Family, Saxifragaceae

More than 1,000 species belong to this family, about 270 of them found in North America. Several of them occur in alpine habitats. The flowers are usually radially symmetrical and have four or five separated petals and four or five stamens. Genera include saxifrages (*Saxifraga*), alumroots (*Heuchera*), foam flowers (*Tiarella*), bishop's-caps (*Mitella*), grasses-of-parnassus (*Parnassia*), mock oranges (*Philadelphus*), hydrangeas (*Hydrangea*), and gooseberries and currants (*Ribes*).

Smartweed Family, Polygonaceae

Although there are only about 800 species in the smartweed family worldwide, more than half of them are found in North America; of these, more than 200 belong to the genus *Eriogonum*. Other genera include smartweeds and knotweeds (*Polygonum*), docks (*Rumex*), sea grapes (*Coccoloba*), and buckwheat (*Fagopyrum*). Some members of the family are recognized by sheaths that encircle the stem at a point where the leaves are attached. None of the flowers has petals, but the sepals are often petal-like.

Snapdragon Family, Scrophulariaceae

There are 3,000 species in the snapdragon family, found throughout the world and on all continents. North America has about 800 species. The family is distinguished by its bilaterally symmetrical flowers with four or five united petals and usually two or four stamens. Common genera include Indian paint brushes (*Castilleja*), beardtongues (*Penstemon*), eyebrights (*Euphrasia*), louseworts (*Pedicularis*), monkey-flowers (*Mimulus*), speedwells (*Veronica*), culver's-roots (*Veronicastrum*), toadflaxes (*Linaria*), and false foxgloves (*Gerardia*). Popular ornamentals include snapdragons (*Antirrhinum*), slipper-flowers (*Calceolaria*), and foxgloves (*Digitalis*).

Spiderwort Family, Commelinaceae

Most of the 500 species in the spiderwort family grow in the tropics and subtropics, but nearly 50 occur in North America. Spiderworts (*Tradescantia*) and day-flowers (*Commelina*) are the most common genera. The family as a whole is distinguished by flowers that have three green sepals and three colored petals.

Spurge Family, Euphorbiaceae

The extremely diverse spurge family consists of about 7,500 species, found in most parts of the world but particularly in the tropics. About 275 species occur in North America. All of them lack petals and have a three-part ovary; many have milky sap, which may have irritant properties. The flowers are radially symmetrical. Among the genera are spurges (*Euphorbia*), crotons (*Croton*), three-seeded mercuries (*Acalypha*), jatrophas (*Jatropha*), tragias (*Tragia*), and nettle spurges (*Cnidoscolus*).

Stick-leaf Family, Loasaceae

Sixty-eight of the 250 species in the stick-leaf family occur in North America; the remainder are found in tropical America. All of them have radially symmetrical flowers with five or ten separated petals and numerous stamens. Most of them have rough hairs. All but eight of the North American species are blazing stars (*Mentzelia*).

St. John's-wort Family, Hypericaceae

About half of the 750 species in this family occur in the tropics. Of the remainder, 57 are found in North America; most of them are St. John's-worts (*Hypericum*). The field marks for this family are the opposite, simple leaves (often with black dots) and the radially symmetrical flowers with five free petals and numerous stamens.

Teasel Family, Dipsacaceae

All 160 species of this family are native to Europe and Asia; only a few have been introduced into North America. Those that do grow on this continent are teasels (*Dipsacus*) and scabiosas (*Scabiosa*). The plants have opposite leaves and bilaterally symmetrical flowers with four or five united petals and four stamens.

Vervain Family, Verbenaceae

More than 2,500 species are in the vervain family, and most are found in the tropics. Many are trees and shrubs, although most of the temperate-zone species are herbs. Ninety-five species occur in North America. They include vervains (*Verbena*), fog-fruits (*Lippia*), glory-bowers (*Clerodendron*), lantanas (*Lantana*), and beauty berries (*Callicarpa*). Most of them have square stems, opposite leaves, bilaterally symmetrical flowers, five united petals, four stamens, and a four-part ovary.

Violet Family, Violaceae

Low-growing violets with pretty flowers are familiar plants to most of us, but it may be surprising to learn that in the tropics, some members of the violet family grow as shrubs or even small trees. Almost all of them have five petals, one of which is frequently prolonged into a spur. There are five stamens. More than 850 species are in the violet family. In North America there are about 80 violets (*Viola*) and three green violets (*Hybanthus*).

Waterleaf Family, Hydrophyllaceae

Members of this family have radially symmetrical flowers with five united petals and five stamens. Of the 300 species in the family, 230 occur in North America, most of them in the western part of the continent. Some of the genera are waterleafs (*Hydrophyllum*), phacelias (*Phacelia*), nemophilas (*Nemophila*), namas (*Nama*), fiesta flowers (*Pholistoma*), eriodictyons (*Eriodictyon*), romanzoffias (*Romanzoffia*), and hesperochirons (*Hesperochiron*).

Water Lily Family, Nymphaeaceae

This completely aquatic family consists of about 90 species, found over much of the world. They are distinguished by their aquatic nature and their flowers, which often have several separated petals and many stamens. North American members of the family include water lilies (*Nymphaea*), spatterdocks (*Nuphar*), watershields (*Brasenia*), and cabombas (*Cabomba*).

Water Lotus Family, Nelumbonaceae

This family consists of three species of pond lilies (*Nelumbo*), one of which is native to North America. These are aquatic plants with huge floating leaves and large solitary flowers. The flowers have many separated petals, many stamens, and a woody fruit with large, sunken seeds.

Water Plantain Family, Alismaceae

The water plantain family lives in water or wet soil throughout the world, but mostly in the Northern Hemisphere. There are about 60 species worldwide, half of which are found in North America. Most of these are arrowheads (*Sagittaria*), water plantains (*Alisma*), and bur-heads (*Echinodorus*). The family is distinguished by its three green sepals, three separated petals (usually white), and six or more stamens.

Wood Sorrel Family, Oxalidaceae

Although there are nearly 1,000 species in the wood sorrel family throughout the world, most of them are tropical. Only the genus *Oxalis* occurs in North America, where it comprises nearly 30 species. Most members of the family have alternate, compound leaves and radially symmetrical flowers with five sepals, five separated petals, and ten stamens.

Collecting and Cultivating Wildflowers

Many botanists prefer to enjoy wildflowers in their natural setting. Most wildflowers do best if they are living in the habitat they are most accustomed to. Most do not last very long after they are picked, and the pretty floral arrangements that can be made with them can be enjoyed only a very short time. Some, like spiderworts, will wither in a few minutes. Of course, there are exceptions, such as the ox-eye daisy, which will look fresh for several hours after being gathered. But often when you pick wildflowers, you are some distance from home, and the length of time needed to transport your beauties back home in a warm vehicle means that most of the flowers are wilted before they ever reach the vase.

On the matter of growing your own wildflower garden, some comments are in order. It is undeniably pleasant to look out a window to a patch of bright wild coreopsis or a carpet of early spring violets, but a great number of wildflowers do not do well in cultivation. Many plants, such as wild orchids and paintbrushes, do very poorly as transplants because they depend on other organisms that live in the native soil where they grow. A lady's-slipper orchid might look attractive the year after it is transplanted, but the chances are slim that the orchid will survive much longer than a couple of years, because certain necessary fungi in the soil will not have survived the transplanting.

If you still have the desire to transplant wildflowers to your home garden, you must make certain that the plant you covet is not an endangered or threatened species. Perhaps as much as 20 percent of the native flora of the United States is rare, with many of the species close to extermination. The chance of the casual wildflower collector's encountering an endangered species may be slim, but the possibility is always present. Where to obtain your wildflowers may be another problem. In many public areas, such as national and state parks and nature preserves, it is illegal to disturb the plant life. If you want to transplant wildflowers from private property, make sure you have the permission of the owner.

To be sure, there are many kinds of common wildflowers that do withstand transplanting very well. Most phloxes usually survive and may even spread after being dug up in the wild and brought to the home garden. Violets and buttercups do marvelously well. Most plants with bulbs or tubers or rhizomes do better than those that have only root systems. Of course, annuals such as blue-eyed Mary will not transplant well, since they will only last out the current year.

Some people believe that because wildflowers do well in the wild without any attention, they will need no attention when set out in the home garden. This may be relatively true once the plant has become established, but the critical times are the few days after transplanting. Transplanted wildflowers should receive the same loving care that you would give a prize dahlia or day lily or larkspur.

One recommended way of establishing a home wildflower garden is to gather the seeds of wildflowers after they have matured. Since different seeds require different treatments, or no treatment at all, you should consult one of the books listed in the suggestions for further reading. These books describe the proper techniques for growing wildflowers from seeds. Rootstocks and bulbs of wildflowers may be purchased from any number of nurseries; for the sake of conservation, however, care should be taken to buy only from nurseries that guarantee that their wildflowers come from nursery-grown stock and are not taken indiscriminantly from the wild. A list of nurseries that sell wildflowers to the general public is published by the New England Wildflower Society, Hemenway Road, Framingham, Mass. 01701.

Wildflower Societies

One of the best ways to learn more about the wildflowers of your area and to meet other people with a love for native plants is to join a wildflower society. Most societies periodically conduct wildflower forays. Each society publishes a newsletter, and many also put out a journal. Some of these organizations are listed below, alphabetically by state.

Alabama Wildflower Society
Box 410
Northport, Ala. 35476

Alaska Native Plant Society
Box 141613
Anchorage, Alaska 99514

Arizona Native Plant Society
Box 41206
Tucson, Ariz. 85717

Arkansas Native Plant Society
Box 36
Roland, Ark. 72135

California Native Plant Society
2380 Ellsworth St., Suite D
Berkeley, Calif. 94704

Colorado Native Plant Society
Box 200
Fort Collins, Colo. 80522

Connecticut Botanical Society
1 Livemore Trail
Killingworth, Conn. 06417

Society of Natural History of
    Delaware
Department of Plant Sciences
University of Delaware
Newark, Del. 19711

Botanical Society of
    Washington
Department of Botany
Smithsonian Institution
Washington, D.C. 20560

Florida Native Plant Society
1203 Orange Ave.
Winter Park, Fla. 32789

Georgia Botanical Society
5890 Long Island Dr., NW
Atlanta, Ga. 30328

Idaho Native Plant Society
Box 9451
Boise, Ida. 83707

Illinois Native Plant Society
Department of Botany
Southern Illinois University
Carbondale, Ill. 62901

Kansas Wildflower Society
Mulvane Art Center
17th & Jewel Sts.
Topeka, Kan. 66621

Kentucky Native Plant Society
Dept. of Biological Sciences
Eastern Kentucky University
Richmond, Ky. 40475

Louisiana Native Plant Society
Rte. 1, Box 151
Saline, La. 71070

Josselyn Botanical Society
Deering Hall
University of Maine
Orono, Maine 04469

New England Wildflower Society
Hemenway Rd.
Framingham, Mass. 01701

Michigan Botanical Club
Botanical Gardens
University of Michigan
Ann Arbor, Mich. 48109

Minnesota Native Plant Society
220 Biological Sciences Center
University of Minnesota
St. Paul, Minn. 55108

Mississippi Native Plant Society
Box EN
Mississippi State, Miss. 39762

Missouri Native Plant Society
Box 6612
Jefferson City, Mo. 65102

Northern Nevada Native Plant
  Society
Box 8965
Reno, Nev. 89507

New Jersey Native Plant
  Society
Frelinghuysen Arboretum
Box 1295R
Morristown, N.J. 07960

Native Plant Society of New
  Mexico
Box 5917
Santa Fe, N.M. 87502

North Carolina Wild Flower
  Preservation Society
North Carolina Botanical
  Garden
University of North Carolina
Chapel Hill, N.C. 27514

Native Plant Society of Ohio
6 Louise Dr.
Chagrin Falls, Ohio 44022

Native Plant Society of Oregon
Department of Biology
Southern Oregon State College
Ashland, Ore. 97520

Pennsylvania Native Plant
  Society
Western Pennsylvania
  Conservancy
316 Fourth Ave.
Pittsburgh, Penn. 15222

Tennessee Native Plant Society
Department of Biology
University of Tennessee
Knoxville, Tenn. 37996

Texas Native Plant Society
Box 23836
TWU Station
Denton, Tex. 76204

Utah Native Plant Society
State Arboretum of Utah
University of Utah
Salt Lake City, Utah 84112

Virginia Wildflower
  Preservation Society
Box 844
Annandale, Va. 22003

Washington Native Plant
  Society
Department of Botany
University of Washington
Seattle, Wash. 98195

West Virginia Native Plant
  Society
West Virginia Natural Heritage
  Program
Box 67
Elkins, W. Va. 26241

Wyoming Native Plant Society
Wyoming Natural Heritage
  Program
1613 Capitol Ave., Room 325
Cheyenne, Wyo. 82001

Glossary

ACHENE—a dry, single-seeded fruit that does not split open at maturity

ALTERNATE—denoting an arrangement of leaves in which the leaves are not situated directly across from each other along the stem (*compare* OPPOSITE)

ANTHER—the part of a stamen that produces pollen

AXIL—the junction of a leaf with the stem

AXILLARY—formed at the point where a leaf joins the stem

BASAL—located at or near the bottom of a plant

BILATERAL SYMMETRY—said of the shape of a flower that can be divided into two equal halves by an imaginary line drawn in only one direction (*compare* RADIAL SYMMETRY)

BIPINNATE—divided once into distinct segments, with each segment in turn divided into smaller distinct segments

BRACT—a structure at the base of a flower, usually leaf-like in appearance

CALYX—the outermost segments of a flower, composed of sepals

COMPOUND—divided more than once; said of a leaf that is divided into leaflets (*compare* SIMPLE)

COROLLA—the segments of a flower just within the calyx, composed of petals

CORONA—a crown of petal-like structures

CYME—a broad, flat arrangement of flowers in which the central flowers bloom first

DISSECTED—divided into small segments

ENTIRE—said of a leaf whose edge has no teeth

EPIPHYTE—a plant that grows on, but does not parasitize, another plant

HERB—a plant that is not woody

HERBACEOUS—referring to a non-woody plant

INFLORESCENCE—a cluster of flowers

LANCEOLATE—lance-shaped; broadest near the base, gradually tapering to the narrower apex

LEAFLET—one unit of a compound leaf

LINEAR—elongated and uniform in width throughout

LOBED—said of a leaf whose edges have notches larger than teeth

OPPOSITE—denoting an arrangement of leaves in which the leaves are situated directly across from each other along the stem (*compare* ALTERNATE)

OVARY—the swollen bottom part of a pistil

OVATE—broadly rounded at the base, becoming narrowed above; broader than lanceolate

PALMATE—divided radiately, like the fingers of a hand

PANICLE—a type of flower cluster composed of several racemes

PAPPUS—cotton-like threads attached to the seeds of flowers (aster family)

PERIANTH—the flower structure including both the calyx (sepals) and the corolla (petals)

PERSISTENT—remaining attached to the plant for a long time

PETAL—one segment of the corolla

PETIOLE—the stalk of a leaf

PINNATE—divided once into distinct segments

PISTIL—the female reproductive structure of a flower, composed of the ovary, style, and stigma

RACEME—a type of flower cluster in which flowers with individual stalks are arranged along an elongated stalk

RADIAL SYMMETRY—said of the shape of a flower that can be divided into two equal halves by an imaginary line drawn in many different directions (*compare* BILATERAL SYMMETRY)

RAY—a petal-like part of a flower head (aster family)

RAY FLOWER—a flower consisting of a petal-like ray (aster family)

RECEPTACLE—that part of the flower to which the perianth, stamens, and pistils are usually attached

RHIZOME—a horizontal underground stem

SAPROPHYTE—a plant that gets its basic nutrients from decaying organic matter

SEPAL—one segment of the calyx, usually green but often of another color and petal-like in appearance

SESSILE—without a stalk

SHEATH—a transparent tissue that encircles the stem at the base of a leaf

SHRUB—a woody plant with several stems of uniform size

SIMPLE—not divided into segments; said of a leaf (*compare* COMPOUND)

SPADIX—a fleshy structure in which flowers are embedded

SPATHE—a large bract that either subtends or encloses a cluster of flowers

SPIKE—a type of flower cluster in which sessile flowers are arranged along an elongated stalk

STAMEN—a male (pollen-producing) structure of a flower, composed of a stalk and an anther

STIGMA—the terminal part of a pistil that receives pollen

STIPULE—a leaf-like structure at the base of a leaf stalk

STYLE—that part of the pistil between the ovary and the stigma

SUBTEND—to lie at the base of something

SUCCULENT—fleshy

TUBE FLOWER—a flower shaped like a tube (aster family)

TUBER—an underground stem, usually swollen with stored food

UMBEL—a type of flower cluster in which the flower stalks arise from the same level

WHORLED—said of leaves or flowers in which three or more are attached at the same point on a stalk

WING—a usually narrow tissue on either side of a stem

Further Reading

Both popular and technical books dealing with the plants of individual states in the U.S.A. are published by state agencies. The popular books are usually illustrated with color photographs and cover only the most common plants. Although the technical books usually cover all of the plants in a given state, most of them are not illustrated, and they use botanical terminology that most lay readers will find baffling.

In addition to this book, there are several regional wildflower books that are well illustrated and that can be of use for wildflower identification. Some are listed below, along with a few books that deal with wildflower gardens.

Regional Guides

Audubon Society Field Guide to North American Wildflowers: Eastern Region. William A. Niering and Nancy C. Olmstead. New York: Knopf, 1979.

Audubon Society Field Guide to North American Wildflowers: Western Region. Richard Spellenberg. New York: Knopf, 1979.

A Field Guide to Pacific States Wildflowers. Theodore F. Niehaus. Boston: Houghton Mifflin, 1976.

A Field Guide to Rocky Mountain Wildflowers. John J. Craighead *et al.* Boston: Houghton Mifflin, 1974.

A Field Guide to Southwestern and Texas Wildflowers. Theodore F. Niehaus. Boston: Houghton Mifflin, 1984.

A Field Guide to Wildflowers of Northeastern and North-Central North America. Roger Tory Peterson and Margaret McKenny. Boston: Houghton Mifflin, 1974.

Newcomb's Wildflower Guide. Lawrence Newcomb. Boston: Little, Brown, 1977. (Covers northeastern and north-central North America.)

Wildflower Gardening

Growing and Propagating Wildflowers. Harry R. Phillips. Chapel Hill, N.C.: University of North Carolina Press, 1985.

Growing Wildflowers: A Cultivator's Guide. Marie Sperka. New York: Scribner, 1984.

The New Wild Flowers and How to Grow Them. Edwin F. Steffek. Beaverton, Ore.: Timber Press, 1983.

The Wildflower Garden. Roy Genders. Chester Springs, Penn.: Dufour Editions, 1977.

Index

Abutilon theophrastii, 142
Acanthaceae, 172
Acanthus Family, 172
Achillea millefolium, 22
Aconitum columbianum, 66
Adder's-tongue, *see* Lily, Yellow Trout
Agastache urticifolia, 110
Agoseris Pale, 136
Agoseris, glauca, 136
Alfalfa, 102
Alismaceae, 186
Allionia incarnata, 80
Allium acuminatum, 82
Allium canadense, 26
Allium cernuum, 82
Amsinckia intermedia, 156
Anaphalis margaritacea, 24
Antelope Horns, Spider, 168
Antennaria plantaginifolia, 24
Antennaria rosea, 76
Apiaceae, 175
Apocynaceae, 175
Apocynum cannabinum, 46
Aquilegia caerulea, 58
Aquilegia canadensis, 114
Aquilegia chrysantha, 138
Araceae, 172
Argemone polyanthemos, 44
Arisaema triphyllum, 170
Aristolochiaceae, 173
Arnica, Heartleaf, 126
Arnica cordifolia, 126
Aroid Family, 172
Arrowhead, 24
Asarum canadense, 166
Asclepiadaceae, 180
Asclepias asperula, 168
Asclepias hirtella, 168
Asclepias incarnata, 98
Asclepias syriaca, 98
Asclepias tuberosa, 118
Aster, Golden, 132
Aster, Heath, 20
Aster, New England, 74

Aster ericoides, 20
Aster Family, 172
Aster novae-angliae, 74
Asteraceae, 172
Astragalus crassicarpus, 100
Aureolaria flava, 164
Avens, Long-plumed, 94
Bachelor's Buttons, 56
Baileya multiradiata, 130
Balsaminaceae, 178
Balsamorhiza sagittata, 124
Balsamroot, Arrowleaf, 124
Barbarea vulgaris, 150
Barberry Family, 173
Beardtongue, Sand, 72
Bear Grass, 28
Beebalm, Lemon, 106
Beeblossom, Scarlet, 104
Beggar-tick, *see* Marigold, Swamp
Bellflower, American, 62
Bellwort, Yellow, 154
Berberidaceae, 173
Bergamot, Wild, 106
Bidens aristosa, 128
Bindweed, 50
Bindweed, Morning-glory, 46
Birthwort Family, 173
Bistort, 40
Bitterroot, 88
Black-eyed Susan, 134
Blackfoot, Gray, 22
Blanket Flower, 112
Blazing Star, 142
Blazing Star, Prairie, 78
Bloodroot, 44
Bluebells, Virginia, 64
Bluebonnet, Texas, 70
Blue-eyed Mary, 72
Boraginaceae, 176
Bouncing Bet, 38
Bouvardia, Trumpet, 120
Bouvardia ternifolia, 120
Brassica campestris, 150
Brassicaceae, 181
Bride's Bonnet, 26

Brodiaea, Elegant, 60
Brodiaea elegans, 60
Buffalo Bur, 158
Bugler, Scarlet, 122
Bunchberry, 32
Bur-reed, 170
Bur-reed Family, 174
Buttercup, Hispid, 144
Buttercup, Large, 148
Buttercup, Tall, 144
Buttercup Family, 174
Butterfly-weed, 118
Buttonweed, 32
Cactaceae, 174
Cactus, Beehive, 84
Cactus, Hedgehog, *see* Cactus,
  Red Claret
Cactus, Rainbow, 84
Cactus, Red Claret, 116
Cactus Family, 174
Caesalpinia Family, 174
Caesalpiniaceae, 174
Calandrinia ciliata, 90
Callirhoe papaver, 94
Calochortus nuttallii, 26
Caltha palustris, 144
Calypso bulbosa, 104
Calyptridium umbellatum, 88
Camas, White, 28
Camassia scilloides, 60
Campanula americana, 62
Campanula rotundifolia, 62
Campanulaceae, 177
Campion, Mexican, 114
Caper Family, 174
Capparidaceae, 174
Cardamine douglasii, 86
Cardinal Flower, 118
Cardinal Flower, Blue, 72
Carduus nutans, 76
Carrot, Wild, 34
Carrot Family, 175
Caryophyllaceae, 182
Cassia fasciculata, 162
Castilleja chromosa, 120
Castilleja indivisa, 120
Castilleja integra, 120
Castilleja occidentalis, 164
Catchfly, Bladder, 38
Cat-tail, Common, 170

Cat-tail Family, 175
Caulophyllum thalictroides, 168
Celandine, *see under* Poppy
Centaurea cyanus, 56
Chelone glabra, 52
Chicory, 56
Chimaphila maculata, 40
Chrysanthemum leucanthemum, see
  Leucanthemum vulgare
Cichorium intybus, 56
Cicuta maculata, 34
Cinquefoil, Sticky, 146
Cinquefoil, Sulphur, 146
Cirsium discolor, 76
Clarkia, Deerhorn, 86
Clarkia pulchella, 86
Claytonia virginica, 36
Cleome serrulata, 102
Clintonia uniflora, 26
Clover, Crimson, 118
Clover, Owl's, 108
Clover, Red, 102
Clover, White, 54
Clover, White Prairie, 54
Clover, Yellow Sweet, 160
Cohosh, Blue, 168
Collinsia verna, 72
Columbine, Blue, 58
Columbine, Wild, 114
Columbine, Yellow, 138
Commelina communis, 66
Commelinaceae, 184
Coneflower, Pale, 74
Coneflower, Yellow, 134
Convolvulaceae, 180
Convolvulus arvensis, 50
Corallorhiza maculata, 104
Coral-root, *see under* Orchid
Coreopsis lanceolata, 126
Cornaceae, 175
Cornus canadensis, 32
Coronilla varia, 100
Coryphantha vivipara, 84
Crane's-bill, Wild, 90
Cress, Pink, 86
Cress, Water, 32
Crownbeard, Winged, 128
Cucurbita foetidissima, 156
Cucurbitaceae, 177
Cypripedium calceolus, 162

195

Daisy, Ox-eye, 20
Dalea candida, 54
Dandelion, Desert, 136
Dandelion, False, 136
Datura stramonium, 48
Daucus carota, 34
Day Lily, *see under* Lily
Day-flower, Common, 66
Deer's Ears, *see* Monument Plant
Delphinium carolinianum, 66
Delphinium tricorne, 66
Dentaria laciniata, 32
Desert Gold, 158
Desert Plume, 150
Dianthus armeria, 92
Diapensia Family, 175
Diapensiaceae, 175
Dicentra canadensis, 52
Dicentra cucullaria, 52
Dicentra uniflora, 52
Dichelostemma pulchellum, 84
Diodia virginiana, 32
Dipsacaceae, 185
Dipsacus fullonum, 80
Dock, *see also* Spatterdock
Dock, Prairie, 124
Dodecatheon meadia, 50
Dogbane, 46
Dogbane Family, 175
Dog-tooth Violet, *see* Lily, Yellow
   Trout
Dogwood Family, 175
Duchesnea indica, 144
Dugaldia hoopesii, 130
Dutchman's Breeches, 52
Echinacea pallida, 74
Echinocereus rigidissimus, 84
Echinocereus triglochidiatus, 116
Elephant Heads, 108
Epilobium angustifolium, 88
Epilobium canum, 122
Erigeron annuus, 20
Erigeron philadelphicus, 74
Eriogonum flavum, 156
Eriophyllum lanatum, 130
Erodium cicutarium, 92
Eryngium yuccifolium, 34
Erythronium americanum, 154
Erythronium grandiflorum, 154
Eschscholtzia californica, 114

Eupatorium coelestinum, 78
Eupatorium fistulosum, 78
Euphorbia corollata, 42
Euphorbia marginata, 42
Euphorbiaceae, 185
Evening Primrose, Common, 152
Evening Primrose, Pink, 88
Evening Primrose Family, 176
Everlasting, Pearly, 24
Feverfew, 22
Fiddle Head, 156
Firepink, 114
Fireweed, 88
Flax, Stiff, 140
Flax, Wild Blue, 58
Flax Family, 176
Fleabane, Annual, 20
Fleabane, Daisy, 74
Flower-of-an-hour, 92
Forget-me-not Family, 176
Four-o'clock, Colorado, 80
Four-o'clock Family, 176
Foxglove, False, 164
Fragaria virginiana, 40
Frasera speciosa, 168
Fritillaria lanceolata, 166
Fritillaria pudica, 154
Fritillary, Yellow, *see* Yellow Bell
Frostweed, 22
Gaillardia pulchella, 112
Galax, 36
Galax aphylla, 36
Garlic, False, 26
Gaura coccinea, 104
Gentian, Soapwort, 64
Gentian Family, 176
Gentiana saponaria, 64
Gentianaceae, 176
Geraniaceae, 177
Geranium, Wild, 90
Geranium carolinianum, 90
Geranium Family, 177
Geranium maculatum, 90
Geum triflorum, 94
Gilia, Blue, 64
Gilia rigidula, 64
Ginger, Wild, 166
Globe Mallow, *see under* Mallow
Goat's-beard, 138
Goldeneye, 128

Goldenrod, Stiff, 134
Goldenrod, Tall, 134
Goldenweed, 124
Gourd Family, 177
Grindelia squarrosa, 132
Ground Plum, 100
Ground-cherry, Smooth, 158
Groundsel, Small's, 136
Gumweed, Common, 132
Gutierrezia sarothrae, 132
Haplopappus acaulis, 124
Harebell, 62
Harebell Family, 177
Hedysarum boreale, 100
Helenium amarum, 128
Helianthus angustifolius, 126
Helianthus annuus, 132
Heliotropium convolvulaceum, 46
Hemerocallis fulva, 112
Hemlock, Water, 34
Hepatica nobilis, 44
Heracleum lanatum, 34
Hesperis matronalis, 86
Heterotheca villosa, 132
Hibiscus, Woolly, 40
Hibiscus lasiocarpus, 40
Hieracium aurantiacum, 112
Hoffmanseggia glauca, 160
Hog Potato, 160
Horsemint, 70
Horsemint, Nettleleaf, 110
Hyacinth, White, 30
Hyacinth, Wild, 60
Hydrophyllaceae, 186
Hydrophyllum capitatum, 96
Hydrophyllum fendleri, 48
Hymenocallis occidentalis, 30
Hypericaceae, 185
Hypericum formosum, 140
Hypericum perforatum, 140
Hypoxis hirsuta, 152
Impatiens capensis, 116
Indian Pipe, 50
Indian Pipe Family, 177
Indian Turnip, *see* Jack-in-the-
    pulpit
Ipomoea hederacea, 64
Ipomoea pandurata, 46
Ipomoea trichocarpa, 98
Ipomopsis longiflora, 62

Iridaceae, 177
Iris, Blue, 60
Iris, Copper, 166
Iris, Dwarf Crested, 60
Iris cristata, 60
Iris Family, 177
Iris fulva, 166
Iris virginica, 60
Ironweed, Baldwin's, 76
Jack-in-the-pulpit, 170
Jewelweed Family, 178
Jimson-weed, 48
Joe-pye-weed, 78
King Devil, 112
Klamath Weed, 140
Lactuca floridana, 56
Lady's Slipper, *see under* Orchid
Lamiaceae, 180
Lamium purpureum, 108
Larkspur, Carolina, 66
Larkspur, Wild, 66
Layia, White, 20
Layia glandulosa, 20
Lettuce, Blue, 56
Leucanthemum vulgare, 20
Lewisia rediviva, 88
Liatris pycnostachya, 78
Ligusticum porteri, 36
Liliaceae, 178
Lilium michiganense, 112
Lily, *see also* Water Lily
Lily, Checker, 166
Lily, Corn, 28
Lily, Orange Day, 112
Lily, Sand, 42
Lily, Sego, 26
Lily, Spider, 30
Lily, Turk's-cap, 112
Lily, Western Fawn, 154
Lily, Yellow Trout, 154
Lily, Zephyr, 30
Lily Family, 178
Linaceae, 176
Linanthus aureus, 158
Linaria dalmatic, 164
Linum lewisii, 58
Linum rigidum, 140
Lithophragma glabra, 38
Lithospermum canescens, 156
Liverleaf, 44

Lizard's Tail, 30
Lizard's Tail Family, 178
Loasaceae, 185
Lobelia cardinalis, 118
Lobelia Family, 178
Lobelia siphilitica, 72
Lobeliaceae, 178
Logania Family, 178
Loganiaceae, 178
Loosestrife, Purple, 82
Loosestrife Family, 179
Lotus, Water, 146
Lotus corniculatus, 160
Lovage, 36
Lungwort, *see* Bluebells, Virginia
Lupine, False, 160
Lupine, Silverstem, 70
Lupinus argenteus, 70
Lupinus texensis, 70
Lygodesmia grandiflora, 74
Lythraceae, 179
Lythrum salicaria, 82
Madder Family, 179
Malacothrix glabrata, 136
Mallow, Desert Globe, 116
Mallow, Narrow-leaved Globe, 116
Mallow, Poppy, 94
Mallow Family, 179
Malvaceae, 179
Marigold, Desert, 130
Marigold, Marsh, 144
Marigold, Swamp, 128
Martynia Family, 179
Martynia proboscidea, 106
Martyniaceae, 179
Mayapple, 42
May-pop, *see* Passion-flower, Purple
Meadow Beauty, Winged, 86
Meadow Beauty Family, 180
Medicago sativa, 102
Melampodium leucanthum, 22
Melastomaceae, 180
Melilotus officinalis, 160
Mentzelia decapetala, 42
Mentzelia laevicaulis, 142
Mertensia virginica, 64
Milfoil, 22
Milkweed, Common, 98

Milkweed, Pink Swamp, 98
Milkweed, Tall Green, 168
Milkweed Family, 180
Milkwort, Pink, 104
Milkwort, Yellow, 162
Milkwort Family, 180
Mimulus alatus, 108
Mimulus guttatus, 164
Mint, *see also* Horsemint
Mint, Slender Mountain, 50
Mint Family, 180
Mirabilis multiflora, 80
Mission Bells, *see* Lily, Checker
Mist Flower, 78
Monarda bradburiana, 70
Monarda citriodora, 106
Monarda fistulosa, 106
Monkey-flower, Blue, 108
Monkey-flower, Yellow, 164
Monkshood, Blue, 66
Monotropa uniflora, 50
Monotropaceae, 177
Monument Plant, 168
Morning Glory, Hairy-fruited, 98
Morning Glory, Ivy-leaved, 64
Morning Glory Family, 180
Mule's Ears, 130
Mullein, Woolly, 158
Mustard Field, 181
Mustard, Family, 150
Nasturtium officinale, 32
Nelumbo lutea, 146
Nelumbonaceae, 186
Nettle, Horse, 48
Nettle, Purple Dead, 108
Nightshade Family, 181
Nothoscordum bivalve, 26
Nuphar luteum, 146
Nyctaginaceae, 176
Nymphaea odorata, 44
Nymphaeaceae, 186
Oenothera biennis, 152
Oenothera fruticosa, 152
Oenothera pilosella, 152
Oenothera speciosa, 88
Onagraceae, 176
Onion, Hooker's, 82
Onion, Nodding, 82
Onion, Wild, 26
Ookow, 84

Opuntia basilaris, 84
Opuntia compressa, 148
Opuntia fragilis, 148
Opuntia phaeacantha, 148
Orchid, Bog Rein, 54
Orchid, Calypso, 104
Orchid, Spotted Coral-root, 104
Orchid, Yellow Lady's-slipper, 162
Orchid Family, 181
Orchidaceae, 181
Orthocarpus purpurascens, 108
Oxalidaceae, 186
Oxalis, Purple, 90
Oxalis stricta, 142
Oxalis violacea, 90
Paintbrush, Desert, 120
Paintbrush, Southwestern, 120
Paintbrush, Texas, 120
Paintbrush, Yellow Mountain, 164
Papaveraceae, 183
Paperflower, *see* Woolly Flower
Papilionaceae, 181
Parsley, Hedge, 36
Parsnip, Cow, 34
Parsnip, Wild, 140
Parthenium integrifolium, 22
Passiflora incarnata, 58
Passifloraceae, 181
Passion-flower, Purple, 58
Passion-flower Family, 181
Pastinaca sativa, 140
Pea, Partridge, 162
Pea Family, 181
Pedicularis groenlandica, 108
Penstemon, Foxglove, 110
Penstemon, Palmer's, 110
Penstemon, Parry's, 122
Penstemon, Pink Plains, 110
Penstemon, Scarlet, 122
Penstemon ambiguus, 110
Penstemon barbatus, 122
Penstemon buckleyi, 72
Penstemon centranthifolius, 122
Penstemon cobaea, 110
Penstemon palmeri, 110
Penstemon parryi, 122
Petunia, Eastern Wild, 62
Petunia, Stalked Wild, 98
Phacelia, Variable, 48
Phacelia heterophylla, 48

Phlox, Eastern, 96
Phlox, Hairy, 96
Phlox Smooth, 96
Phlox, White, 46
Phlox diffusa, 46
Phlox divaricata, 96
Phlox Family, 182
Phlox glaberrima, 96
Phlox pilosa, 96
Physalis subglabrata, 158
Phytolacca americana, 38
Phytolaccaceae, 183
Pickerelweed, 70
Pickerelweed Family, 182
Pink, *see also* Firepink
Pink, Deptford, 92
Pink, Indian, 118
Pink, Marsh, 94
Pink, Rush, 74
Pink Family, 182
Pink Windmills, 56
Pitcher Plant, Yellow, 138
Pitcher Plant Family, 182
Platanthera dilatata, 54
Podophyllum peltatum, 42
Pokeweed, 38
Pokeweed Family, 183
Polemoniaceae, 182
Polygala lutea, 162
Polygala sanguinea, 104
Polygalaceae, 180
Polygonaceae, 184
Polygonum amphibium, 92
Polygonum bistortoides, 40
Pontederia cordata, 70
Pontederiaceae, 182
Poppy, California, 114
Poppy, Celandine, 150
Poppy, White Prickly, 44
Poppy Family, 183
Poppy Mallow, *see under* Mallow
Portulaca Family, 183
Portulacaceae, 183
Potentilla glandulosa, 146
Potentilla recta, 146
Prickly Pear, Beavertail, 84
Prickly Pear, Cliff, 148
Prickly Pear, Common, 148
Prickly Pear, Small, 148
Prickly Poppy, *see under* Poppy

199

Primrose, *see also* Evening Primrose
Primrose, Parry's, 100
Primrose Family, 183
Primula parryi, 100
Primulaceae, 183
Prunella vulgaris, 106
Psilostrophe tagetina, 124
Puccoon, 156
Pussy Paws, 88
Pussytoes, 24
Pussytoes, Pink, 76
Pycnanthemum tenuifolium, 50
Pyrola Family, 183
Pyrolaceae, 183
Pyrrhopappus carolinianus, 136
Queen Anne's Lace, 34
Railroad Vine, 156
Ranunculaceae, 174
Ranunculus acris, 144
Ranunculus hispidus, 144
Ranunculus macranthus, 148
Ratibida columnifera, 134
Rattlesnake Master, 34
Red Maids, 90
Rhexia virginica, 86
Rocket, Purple, 86
Rocket, Yellow, 150
Rosaceae, 184
Rose Family, 184
Rosinweed, 126
Rubiaceae, 179
Rudbeckia hirta, 134
Ruellia caroliniensis, 62
Ruellia pedunculata, 98
Sabatia angularis, 94
Sage, Wild, 72
Sagittaria latifolia, 24
Salvia lyrata, 72
Sanguinaria canadensis, 44
Saponaria officinalis, 38
Sarracenia flava, 138
Sarraceniaceae, 182
Saururaceae, 178
Saururus cernuus, 30
Saxifraga flagellaris, 142
Saxifragaceae, 184
Saxifrage, Yellow, 142
Saxifrage Family, 184
Scrophulariaceae, 184
Self-heal, 106

Senecio anonymus, 136
Shooting Star, 50
Sidalcea, Oregon, 94
Sidalcea oregana, 94
Silene cucubalus, 38
Silene laciniata, 114
Silene virginica, 114
Silphium integrifolium, 126
Silphium terebinthinaceum, 124
Sisymbrium linearifolium, 56
Skunk Cabbage, 170
Smartweed, Scarlet, 92
Smartweed Family, 184
Smilacina racemosa, 28
Snakeweed, 132
Snapdragon Family, 184
Sneezeweed, Narrow-leaved, 128
Sneezeweed, Orange, 130
Snow-on-the-Mountain, 42
Solanaceae, 181
Solanum carolinense, 48
Solanum rostratum, 158
Solidago canadensis, 134
Solidago rigida, 134
Solomon's Seal, False, 28
Sonchus oleraceus, 138
Sparganiaceae, 174
Sparganium eurycarpum, 170
Spatterdock, 146
Sphaeralcea ambigua, 116
Sphaeralcea angustifolia, 116
Spider-flower, Prairie, 102
Spiderwort, Common, 58
Spiderwort, Tall, 78
Spiderwort Family, 184
Spigelia marilandica, 118
Spring Beauty, 36
Spurge, Flowering, 42
Spurge Family, 185
Squirrel-corn, 52
Stanleya pinnata, 150
Star-grass, Yellow, 152
Steer's Head, 52
Stick-leaf, *see also* Blazing Star
Stick-leaf Family, 185
Stork's-bill, 92
Strawberry, Indian, 144
Strawberry, Wild, 40
Streptopus roseus, 82
Stylophorum diphyllum, 150

St. John's-wort, *see also* Klamath Weed
St. John's-wort, Scouler's, 140
St. John's-wort Family, 185
Sundrops, Common, 152
Sundrops, Prairie, 152
Sunflower, Common, 132
Sunflower, Narrow-leaved, 126
Sweet Potato Vine, Wild, 46
Sweet William, *see* Phlox, Eastern
Symplocarpus foetidus, 170
Talinum calycinum, 92
Teasel, 80
Teasel Family, 185
Thermopsis montana, 160
Thistle, Field, 76
Thistle, Nodding, 76
Thistle, Sow, 138
Tickseed, 126
Toadflax, Dalmatian, 164
Toothwort, Common, 32
Torilis japonica, 36
Touch-me-not, Spotted, 116
Tradescantia ohiensis, 78
Tradescantia virginiana, 58
Tragopogon dubius, 138
Trefoil, Bird's-foot, 160
Trifolium incarnatum, 118
Trifolium pratense, 102
Trifolium repens, 54
Trillium, Red, 166
Trillium, White, 24
Trillium flexipes, 24
Trillium recurvatum, 166
Triteleia hyacinthina, 30
Trout Lily, *see under* Lily
Trumpet, Hummingbird, 122
Trumpet-flower, Long-flowered, 62
Turtlehead, White, 52
Twisted-stalk, Rosy, 82
Typha latifolia, 170
Typhaceae, 175
Umbrella-plant, Yellow, 156
Umbrella-wort, 80
Unicorn Plant, 106
Uvularia grandiflora, 154
Velvetleaf, 142
Veratrum californicum, 28
Verbascum thapsus, 158
Verbena, Wild, 80

Verbena canadensis, 80
Verbenaceae, 185
Verbesina alternifolia, 128
Verbesina virginica, 22
Vernonia baldwinii, 76
Vervain Family, 185
Vetch, American, 102
Vetch, Crown, 100
Vetch, Northern Sweet, 100
Vetch, Winter, 68
Vicia americana, 102
Vicia villosa, 68
Viguiera multiflora, 128
Viola adunca, 68
Viola pedata, 68
Viola pubescens, 162
Viola sororia, 68
Viola striata, 54
Violaceae, 186
Violet, Bird's-foot, 68
Violet, Dog-tooth, *see* Lily, Yellow Trout
Violet, Spreading Blue, 68
Violet, White, 54
Violet, Woolly Blue, 68
Violet, Yellow, 162
Violet Family, 186
Wake Robin, *see* Trillium, Red
Water Lily, 44
Water Lily Family, 186
Water Lotus Family, 186
Water Plantain Family, 186
Watercress, *see* Cress, Water
Waterleaf, Capitate, 96
Waterleaf, Fendler's, 48
Waterleaf Family, 186
Wintergreen, Spotted, 40
Wood Sorrel, Yellow 142
Wood Sorrel Family, 186
Woodland Star, Smooth, 38
Woolly Flower, 124
Wyethia amplexicaulis, 130
Xerophyllum tenax, 28
Yarrow, 22
Yarrow, Golden, 130
Yellow Bell, 154
Zauschneria sp., *see under* Epilobium
Zephyranthes atamasco, 30
Zigadenus elegans, 28

Credits

Photographs are identified by page number and sequence of description (a, b, c, d) in the text facing the plate.
All photographs not credited are by the author.

David H. Askegaard 104b; Carolyn Collier Bates 40a; Joan Boudreau 21b; Stephen M. Bowling 164c; Ann C. Cooper 156a; Joe F. Duft 28b, 28d, 34d, 48a, 66c, 74d, 76a, 100c, 102d, 104c, 108c, 110d, 124d, 126a, 130b, 140d, 146a, 148d, 154c, 160b, 164a; Debbie Rymal Folkerts 138c; William Follette 20d, 24b, 26d, 68b, 88c, 90d, 136b, 136c, 142a, 156b, 166b; Walter K. Graf 156d; Milo Guthrie 136a; Karen Sue Haller 92a; Linda Hardie-Scott 30b, 122c; Jessie M. Harris 36d, 64c, 86d, 108b, 162d; Elizabeth L. Horn 28c; Rob L. Jacobs 82b, 82c, 126d; Doug Ladd 86b, 100d; Frank A. Lang 158a; David Mueller 84d, 122d; David Northington 160a; Nancy and Bill Piper 150c; Marvin Poulson 26a, 38a, 46c, 48b, 54d, 60d, 82a, 84a, 96a, 100a, 110a, 110b, 116c, 120b, 124b, 128a, 130d; George C. Pyne, Jr. 44b; R. W. Redfield 46d, 52a, 88d; Bob Reeves 120c; Simpson & Co. Nature Stock 40d; Paul Somers 54a; Bob Steele 52c, 70a, 84b, 94b, 114d, 142d, 154b; W. Carl Taylor 58b, 86c, 144a, 168d, 170a; Steve L. Timme 42c, 60b, 94c, 106a, 110c; Tom C. Ulrich 50b; R. C. Whitmore 140b, 148a; Margaret J. Williams 84c; Robert G. Young 36a, 80b, 130a.

Line drawings of botanical subjects by Mark Mohlenbrock.
Range map adapted from U.S. Department of Agriculture original.

About the Author

ROBERT H. MOHLENBROCK, one of the premier botanists in North America, is Distinguished Professor of Botany at Southern Illinois University at Carbondale, where he has taught since 1957. A Fellow of the Illinois State Academy of Science, he is the author of more than 30 books on botanical subjects, including ten volumes in the series *The Illustrated Flora of Illinois* (Southern Illinois University Press) and *Where Have All the Wildflowers Gone?* (Macmillan, 1983). He serves as a consultant to the U.S. Forest Service, U.S. Fish and Wildlife Service, and Illinois Department of Conservation. In 1986 he was named North American chairman for botany of the Species Survival Commission of the International Union of Conservation of Nature and Natural Resources.

Professor Mohlenbrock's areas of special interest and research extend to taxonomy, nomenclature, ornamental plants, rare and endangered species of plants, and botanical conservation. His field trips have taken him to several continents, and he is an active lecturer to many conservation organizations, civic groups, and garden clubs. Since 1984 he has written a monthly column on the national forests of the United States for the magazine *Natural History*.

Other books in the authoritative, highly popular
Macmillan Field Guide Series
are available at your local bookstore or by mail.
To order directly, return the coupon below to

MACMILLAN PUBLISHING COMPANY
Special Sales Department
866 Third Avenue
New York, New York 10022

Line Sequence	ISBN	Author/Title	Price	Quantity
1	0020796501	Dunlop: ASTRONOMY, paperback	$ 8.95	_____
2	002063370X	Moody: FOSSILS, paperback	$ 8.95	_____
3	0020796404	Bell/Wright: ROCKS AND MINERALS, paperback	$ 8.95	_____
4	0020796609	Bull: BIRDS OF NORTH AMERICA, paperback	$ 9.95	_____
5	0025182307	Bull: BIRDS OF NORTH AMERICA, hardcover	$19.95	_____
6	002063420X	Mohlenbrock: WILDFLOWERS, paperback	$ 9.95	_____
7	0025854402	Mohlenbrock: WILDFLOWERS, hardcover	$24.95	_____
8	0020137001	Dunlop: WEATHER AND FORECASTING, paperback	$ 9.95	_____

Sub-total $ _____

Please add postage and handling costs--$1.00 for the first book
and 50¢ for each additional book $ _____

Total $ _____

_____ Enclosed is my check/money order payable to Macmillan Publishing Co.

_____ Bill my _____ MasterCard _____ Visa Card # _____

Expiration date _____ Signature _____
                                    -- Charge orders valid only with signature

Control No. [_____]   Order Type [Reg]   Lines [_____]   Units

Ship to: _____   Bill to: _____

_____   _____

_____   _____

_____ Zip Code   _____ Zip Code

For information regarding bulk purchases, please write to Special Sales Director
at the above address. Publisher's prices are subject to change without notice.
Offer good January 1, 1987, through January 1, 1988. Allow 3 weeks for delivery.
                                                                    FC# 427

Field Notes

Field Notes